A COMMUNIST'S JOURNEY

To Moscow And Beyond

William Briggs

Copyright © 2025 by William Briggs

All rights reserved.

ISBN: 978-0-646-71568-1 print

ISBN: 978-0-646-71569-8 ebook

Contents

Introduction 1

1 The muddle that is the left 10
2 The stumbling path to the SPA 31
3 The Fourth Congress and commitment 60
4 And so, to the Soviet Union 91
5 Making a new start... 132
6 Looking for 'home'... 159
7 Not the end: just another part of the journey 188

Also by William Briggs

Tomorrow's People Progress Publishers 1988

Classical Marxism in an Age of Capitalist Crisis: the past is prologue Routledge 2019

Removing the Stalin Stain: Marxism and the working class in the 21st century Zero Books 2020

A Cauldron of Anxiety: capitalism in the twenty-first century Zero Books 2021

China, the USA and Capitalism's Last Crusade: when survival is all that matters Zero Books 2021

For all those who have fought for the future. For those who are fighting for that future and for those who will make that future a reality.

Introduction

'If I were you, I'd give it away.' It was meant to be funny. But it was also meant to belittle and to ridicule. It was an awkward, almost embarrassed way of putting someone in his place. It's what people do to those that express ideas that are not the ideas of the *status quo*. It was said, on television, to a communist. It could have been said to any communist in any age, in any setting, anywhere in Australia.

The 'clever' line came from the mouth of comedian and actor Paul Hogan. He was a guest on a television talk show, now lost in the mist of time, and probably rightly so. The other guest was Frank Hardy. The interviewer had asked Hardy what he had achieved in his years in the Communist Party of Australia. Hardy spoke of his involvement in the nine-year long strike of Aboriginal workers at Wave Hill cattle station. Hogan went for the cheap laugh. Hardy pointed out that the strikers had won and that the call for land rights and recognition had taken a big step forward as a result.

'What have you achieved?' What have I? It is a question that could haunt you but should not. I am a communist. There is absolutely nothing special about that. In the last century, many thousands of men and women in this country have become communists. Some for a short time but others have stayed the course. Some, like myself, have left the movement for a time and then returned. Communists are not in any respect special. Some have led outstanding lives and have been beacons to others, but it is not the individual man or woman who is special but rather the ideas that motivate them. The ideas of Marx, Engels and Lenin are ideas that shaped the world and remain as relevant and fresh today as when the working class first heard them. The idea of personal achievement, of material gain, fame, fortune or notoriety is not a motivating factor, but it is intrinsically locked into the mindset of the ideology that communists always fight against. What have you achieved? What do you do? How much are you worth?

Several decades ago, an American communist spoke to a small group of his comrades when he was 'retiring' from full-time Party work. It is an odd concept. Communists do not 'retire' from the world, or from the struggle that drives them. He spoke of his life and how, according to the norms of capitalist society he had achieved little. He made light of this. He

INTRODUCTION

laughed and said that he was 'retiring' with a suit of clothes, a small rented apartment, and enough money in his bank account to pay his rent and keep him alive. The capitalist dream, he said, was to accumulate wealth. He was, he said, far wealthier than when he had arrived, as a naked and penniless baby. He had remained steadfast to a belief system. He was not able to make a revolution. None of us can. We cannot, as if by magic, create class consciousness in the working class. We cannot conjure up the conditions that will see the scales fall from their eyes, and by realising their power relegate capitalism to the dust bin of history. The task of the communist in conditions such as ours is to work patiently, to explain, to offer leadership, to educate, to agitate and to play some part in the organisation of the class. Inch by inch, step by step, as laborious as it always is, that work can and will bear fruit. Everyone who is a communist was influenced by someone or some action. That is how class consciousness builds, until the mass of the working class fully appreciate that they hold the potential for power in their hands.

We can only keep faith with an idea and do whatever, whenever and wherever we can to convince the working class that they are the ones who can, will, and must change the world.

This is exactly why the Hogans of our world deliver those cheap shots. To acknowledge the strength that comes from belief in the cause of Marxism-Leninism, is to acknowledge the weakness and lack of purpose that capitalist society engenders in the people. So, the apologists of a system that tears down and destroys must ridicule and denigrate. The opposing 'idea' must never be able to breathe. The state ensures that this will be the case. It requires no thought. It makes life simple.

To hold fast to beliefs, to fight when victory seems impossible, makes the communist a figure of ridicule but also one to be secretly envied. It is often a cold place on the outskirts of society but there is comfort in knowing that you, I, we, share something that is unbreakable. My wife and comrade Rose once told me that a good friend of hers had admitted that she wished she had the belief that Rose clearly had. A seemingly small thing, but an important declaration, just the same.

A memoir is written or I think should be written, with more than a hint of reluctance. A memoir can so easily be seen as an end point; the drawing of a line under a life. This is certainly not the case, or at least I hope not. I would like to think that there is still a little left in the tank and that, even ineffectually in the eyes of the Paul Hogans among us, I can still take some small part in the struggle for a better world.

I first consciously thought of myself as a socialist in 1971. That is a long time ago. The journey has been a haphazard one.

INTRODUCTION

The belief in socialism, in a better world, in a world free of capitalism remains. The young man that I was made the claim to be a Marxist. I had very little appreciation of what that meant. My reading was sparse. My comrades read as little as I did. This state of affairs went on for year after year. Generations of communists in this country managed to dodge theory and it shows.

This memoir is partly reminiscence and partly an observation of what can go wrong when theory is 'dodged', ignored, or incorrectly applied. Communists do not come fully formed. They grow, but often in some very arid soil. I look at the left today and can see the results of a lack of theory. I believe it to be a tragedy. If unchecked, the proud movement for socialism will suffer further setbacks. This might sound unduly pessimistic and it probably is. The idea for which those thousands have struggled is undented by poor application. Capitalism has delivered us all into a very dark place. Yes, things are in a poor state but that need not be the case. So, the reminiscences, the observations, the semi-historical narrative cannot but be infused with theory.

The movement for socialism, and its embodiment in the Marxist-Leninist Party has had moments of upsurge and of decline. It has lurched from crisis to crisis, swung from sectarianism to right opportunism and has rested more often in the camp of right opportunism and with it the perpetual threat of liquidation. Today is something of a nadir for much of the traditional Marxist movement in Australia.

Is this turning away from theory and a fuller, richer appreciation of Marxist thought that has so long plagued political life in Australia, an inevitable consequence of living in a country deeply imbued with anti-intellectualism? Has the inability of the communist movement to make serious inroads into mainstream Australian political life and culture made the idea of sacrifice anathema to intellectuals? Some writers have decried the Communist Party, in various periods, as being populated with mediocre minds. The sad reality is that in the past decades, just as capitalism was entering a new and sharper crisis, the communist movement weakened. The paucity of ideas, so prevalent in the broader society, is reflected in the dwindling ranks of communists. Those entering the Communist Party of Australia today are barely troubled by any calls to study, to comprehend what it is to be a communist, or how the battle of ideas might be fought out. The working class has become a vague concept, to be supported by the trade union movement. Political focus, such as it is, is directed to broad social movements and the politics of identity.

INTRODUCTION

Is the writing on the wall? Is it time to return to those dispiriting words of Paul Hogan and 'give it away?' the answer must be a resounding no! Marxism and its political expression in the form of a Marxist-Leninist Party has never been destroyed and nor shall it. This or that Party might implode, become a victim of a set of ideological errors that lead it to liquidation but the idea remains and there are those who are prepared to fight for that idea. Their numbers might be reduced but the catastrophic crisis of capitalism demands that a renaissance, a re-birth, but more importantly a continuation and re-growth of the Marxist-Leninist Party continues. Sadly, the Communist Party of Australia has irretrievably lost its way. That is not an end of things. The banner, the torch, simply gets taken up again. Such a party already exists. It has an optimism that stems from an understanding of the tasks ahead, why those tasks must be met and an optimism which flows from understanding, appreciating and directing theory to the mass struggle. How successful it will be in avoiding the same pitfalls of its predecessor will depend, not on its cadre alone, but on its capacity to maintain a commitment to the ideology that it espouses. It was formed from leading cadre from the Communist Party of Australia who, after fighting the good fight for so long, accepted that the CPA was, in all but name, finished.

A COMMUNIST'S JOURNEY

My life has reflected the trials and tribulations, the travails of the movement within which I have moved and lived. I have been neither a mover nor a shaker, but rather I have been moved and I have been shaken. Looking back, I must admit that I got more things wrong than right. I am not alone in this. It can hardly be a surprise when all of us who have called ourselves communist have lived in a sea of bourgeois thinking and have struggled in a movement that has infrequently been able to counter that tidal wave of ideology. All of us, individuals and parties alike often got it wrong. Such is life.

My almost fifty-five years in and around the communist movement reflect the defeats, the mistakes, the errors of judgement and of the lack of clarity that has marked that movement. My life is not the subject of these pages. It has not been, in any way special. It is not a life to be remembered. I have achieved little. Even so, I would reject the attempted laugh line of Paul Hogan. I joined a political movement when I was still 17 years old. I had no real idea of what I was doing, apart from an almost unconscious response to a vague awareness that things were wrong. I awkwardly approached this movement. I had no theory to fall back on, just that unconscious feeling that the people deserved something better. More than half a century

INTRODUCTION

later, I believe that things are wrong and must be made better. I hope that those fifty years have taught me some things. I hope that I can recognise my mistakes and the mistakes that political organisations can and do make.

Political mistakes, frequent misinterpretation of ideas, a lack of theoretical and ideological clarity, have left the communist movement in Australia and around the world weakened and wounded. The ideas that motivated me and still do, have not been extinguished by these stumbling and poor manifestations of theory and practice. An old union activist once said, 'it's not how many times they knock you down that matters, it's how many times you get up.' It is a sad reflection of how the movement has operated. Sometimes it has been knocked down and sometimes it has, through an inability or unwillingness to attend to theory, knocked itself down, but the idea is still there. The ideology that drives the idea is more relevant than ever. The need for a strong, ideologically literate Marxist-Leninist Party is more urgent than ever as capitalism devours all and itself.

What follows is not a chronology of a life but a personalised history of a movement. It is not the drawing of a line under a life, but the turning of a page.

Chapter One

The muddle that is the left

At last count there were five political parties in Australia that have their roots in the tradition of orthodox Marxism, or rather Marxism-Leninism. Those that come from a broadly Trotskyist heritage number at least 20. The ever-growing alphabet soup of the left tells us something. The split, counter split, the odd half-hearted attempt at reformation and then further split is accelerating as the crisis that is engulfing capitalism widens. As capitalism hurtles toward collapse, the Marxist left appears to be weakening. Why?

Anyone who has ever been part of the organised Marxist left, regardless of party allegiance will at some time have been asked the same question; why can't you all get together? You all want the same thing. It is an appealing question and of course it would be nice and nicer still if it were a simple matter.

THE MUDDLE THAT IS THE LEFT

From time-to-time statements are issued, calls for 'left unity' and such-like are made. There have been attempts, both from the orthodox Marxist world and from the Trotskyist or former Trotskyist groups to form alliances. They have all ended in failure. Egos certainly come into conflict with each other. I remember a former friend and comrade of mine implacably stating that 'this behaviour would not be tolerated in any party I run.' I don't remember the 'behaviour' she was alluding to but the problem of egos crowding together in a fairly confined political space has remained deeply fixed in my memory.

But it is not as simple as sheer human frailty or folly. The struggle for Marxism-Leninism is a struggle of ideas. It must always remain an absolute necessity to 'get things right.' If you don't then the shelf life of the party, or group, or movement, will always be a short one.

Recognising that you have things 'right' is no easy matter. It is always fraught with problems. The best we can hope for is to get the theory in place before committing too many mistakes in practice. What we have, today, is a left in crisis.

In considering my own life on the left I have felt compelled to consider this crisis. For anybody seriously contemplating the history of the movement for socialism, or for anybody engaged in the day-to-day struggle of the left and communist movement, it is necessary to answer that question, why? Legions of men and women have been drawn into the fight against capitalism. The MCG could be filled and refilled with those who have joined, travelled for a time, and got off the train, a few stops short of their desired destination. Again, the question arises as to why the political 'dead' are so many. I have been among the casualties.

People join the Party for all the best and most noble of reasons. Something drives too many away. Is it the smallness of membership and the seemingly impossible tasks ahead? Is it a clash of personalities, so rife in a small organisation? Is it the social isolation and alienation from the broader society that many feel with intensity after the initial rush of excitement and enthusiasm wanes? It's all of this and more. The answer as to why this is so and why the left has fragmented, so obviously and to its own detriment, are linked. The Party is strong when it has a cadre that is not just committed but steeped in the theory of Marxism-Leninism and able to teach that theory in a rich and meaningful way to the membership. When that is in place then it is possible to influence the class that will effect change. Sadly, this infusion of theory has never really happened. That might sound harsh, but too much political blood has been shed in splits and woefully incorrect interpretations of theory. The

Party has swung from left sectarianism to right opportunism. Opportunist politics have dominated and within opportunism lies the seeds of destruction and liquidation.

Each new group that emerges on the political horizon comes with the promise that it has a claim to a correct application of theory. Some get a foothold, others wither and die, only to be replaced by new groups and grouplets, hydra-like, determined to confront capitalism, but more often to confuse those seeking answers.

It is the search for answers that brought me back to the movement, and back to the Party. I left the old Socialist Party of Australia (SPA) before it re-took the name Communist Party of Australia (CPA). I had always felt myself a socialist and bandied the term Marxist about but with no real authority to do so. My theoretical education had been poor but so too had that of the majority of my comrades. There were some who fared better than others but things have always been a bit 'hit-and-miss' in this regard. When I joined, (or is it re-joined) the CPA I found that what had been a poor attention to Party education had not improved. On the contrary, it has worsened. There can be no excuse and none was ever offered.

I felt a sense of disappointment in this. I had hoped for better but it was, in retrospect, a foolish hope.

The few years prior to my return to the Party were years of rather intense study. I don't mean that I took myself off to a quiet spot and read Marx and Lenin from cover-to cover. It wasn't to prepare myself for membership. I had no notion of where I was headed. I had just retired from work as a teacher and time hung heavily on me. Rose suggested that I should look at a return to study. So, I looked about and found that I could do a Master of International Relations, as an on-line student. One of my lecturers told us that to avoid becoming swamped in ideas we should pick one of the three dominant schools of thought and stick with it. The choice between, Liberalism, Realism, or Marxism was an easy one to make. What I discovered was that within Marxism, there were subsets and subsets within the subsets. None of them had much relevance beyond an academic pursuit but it did reveal just how disputed the theory had become. It shone a light, at first dimly, on why the crisis in capitalism was not being challenged. Marxist theory had become so removed from practice as to make it laughable.

The MA was able to be completed. It allowed me to write a PhD thesis which was about the crisis in Marxism and how that crisis unconsciously aided and abetted the continued existence of capitalism. I finished the thesis, pressed send and waited.

THE MUDDLE THAT IS THE LEFT

It was in late 2017 that the email arrived. It contained, among other things, detailed comments or reviews of the thesis from the readers or assessors. One set of remarks was particularly perceptive. The reader had said that my work was more an attempt at clarifying ideas in the mind of the author and less an academic thesis. I was at first annoyed. When the dust had settled and after I was let into that little club of PhD awardees, I reconsidered those words. He was quite right. It was an attempt at clarifying, in my own mind, what Marxism was and was not and more importantly, how this related to the practice of Marxism in the context of the working-class activist party. I had never seen the thesis quite in that light. I had no concept that within a couple of short years I would be seeking membership of the Communist Party of Australia.

My return to the ranks of the CPA was via a slightly circuitous route. The years of study led me to something of a flirtation with 'orthodox' Trotskyism and from there to a brief time with the Socialist Alliance (a former Trotskyist Party) that is an interesting hybrid creature. It is part ecological, part left Green Party, part broad socialist, and part left social-democrat. Some members regard themselves as revolutionary socialists, some shy away from such an 'extreme' label. Some see themselves as Marxists while others see Marxism as one contributing idea.

It ends up being neither fish nor fowl. My time with them was brief and frustrating.

Not long after our paths diverged, I returned to the SPA (now CPA). I use both sets of initials deliberately. I had a nostalgic belief that I was 'coming home.' In a sense I was, but the foundations of that home had been let go and had long since crumbled, the paintwork was shabby, the brickwork needed re-pointing and the roof needed replacing. I had been reading the paper, *The Guardian*, on and off for years. In the lead-up to my return I had been writing occasional pieces for on-line magazines. A couple of these articles were re-printed by *The Guardian*. I had no problem with that. A former comrade from the old days suggested to the editor of the paper that I ought to be sounded out about having these articles re-printed. I made contact with the editor and began to send the odd piece directly to the paper. One thing led to another and some months later I became, once more a member.

The briefest of retrospectives and a moment of introspection

Life and the direction a life might take is rarely a carefully plotted, planned and executed journey. Plans are seldom made.

THE MUDDLE THAT IS THE LEFT

Things just happen. A chance encounter, picking up that book on that particular day, an overheard conversation, a newspaper article, a random decision to go to a film or a concert or a rally can so easily alter the course of a life. We don't often like to confess this but I feel it to be true. Now there are obviously a couple of riders to this. People are not simply blown like chaff in the wind. Something deep below the surface, often unknown to you at the time, triggers a reaction. Socialists, communists, do not emerge from some chrysalis, ready formed. But the unformed, uninformed mind, will reject that which other people will adopt and hold fast to ideas that are scorned by others and often the majority.

This is pretty much how my own journey began. There were certainly no strong influences or childhood role models, no discussions of ideas over the dinner table, but things happened. Life happened.

I can now look back on a life that has taken various turns and can only hope that each turn was made with the best of intentions. This does not mean that I have not regretted some of the twists along the way.

In this introspective frame of mind, I will lay out, in a vague chronology, some of those turns, some of the forks in the road. It won't start at the beginning because it is not the story of one life but rather the way that life, politics and events have framed and formed a life. But before we get too far down this road, it's as well to skim across some of the issues that will follow.

I had left the Party after working for it for five years as a full-time functionary. I had been part of a small group in Hobart who formed, or rather re-formed a branch of the SPA. I had been chosen to be the secretary of that branch. Not long after the Fourth Congress of the Party, Rose and I were sent to Moscow for three years. I was to take up the role of correspondent for the then *Socialist* which was later renamed *The Guardian*. This was during the early1980s. We left Moscow soon after Mikhail Gorbachev became the leader of the USSR. It was only a matter of a few years before the USSR was no more. That historical moment, combined with a rather serious rift between the SPA and the International Department of the Communist Party of the Soviet Union meant that I was not replaced and so became the last to hold that post and with the passing of time have become the only surviving Australian communist to have worked as a correspondent in Moscow.

When we returned to Australia, I began work with the *Guardian* and Rose in the Party bookshop. I was a little disoriented by the process. Settling back into bourgeois Australia was not easy. I began to find myself in conflict with the Party leadership. I tried to convince myself that there was an ideological component to this. Some in the leadership put it down to a strong current of individualism on my part stemming from the influence of bourgeois ideology and a lack of Party discipline. In retrospect, I believe that they were mostly, if not entirely, correct. It does beg the question of how deep was my understanding of the theory that was the basis of the Party. If I am honest, and this is the time for honesty, then most assuredly my knowledge was flawed. And limited. It is hardly a defence to say that I was not alone in this. Theoretical development and any real sense of ideological clarity were spread thinly. Sadly, since my re-joining the Party, I have seen no improvement in this state of affairs. On the contrary, it seems to be even worse.

My problems with the Party did reflect a degree of eclecticism on my part. I lacked the consistency of thought that a deep understanding of Marxist-Leninist theory and practice can offer. This was partly my fault and partly the fault of the Party that was also proving to be just a little eclectic in its approach. It spoke of the need to develop cadres and yet Party education was poorly and erratically handled. The then General-Secretary, Peter Symon, at the time of the Fourth Congress and a split in the SPA once said to me that it would be good if he could cease all Party work for 12 months and instead put all members to work studying the theory that was so lacking. He lamented what he saw as a lack of ideological rigour and he saw the desperate need to develop cadres. It was said in an unguarded moment in our flat in Moscow. He obviously knew it could never be. It seemed to me that he was as close to a fully developed communist as I have met in Australia. He fought against right opportunism and briefly won. He fought simultaneously for Marxism-Leninism against both left sectarianism and opportunism but even before his death and before his time as leader was over, the Party was clearly on an opportunist path once more.

The life of an individual can be seen as almost a microcosm of that of an entire organisation. This is not said to elevate the individual nor to reduce the organisation but my own trajectory has been marked by error and of correction. That might possibly be a case of wishful thinking. After each correction, new problems, and new mistakes were committed. As it is with the individual, then so too with an organisation. It might be seen as a constant battle between left and right, although sometimes an unconscious battle. This very lack of consciousness marks out much of the problem. Seeing the problem in others can sometimes mean ignoring the problem with the individual and his or her closest comrades.

The movement for socialism in this country, and around the world has been marked very much by just such a tendency to swing between left and right. Perhaps, a little more attention to laying the foundations, paying attention to what is needed might turn the 'unconscious' into the conscious. It's all about getting it right, while making sure that getting it right is not caught up in subjectivity.

Getting it Right

If the struggle against capitalism is to have any chance of success, and succeed it must, then it is essential to 'get it right.' This is as important for the individual as it is for the organisation. It is doubly so when the movement for socialism has been so appallingly served by those calling themselves Marxists for so very long. I am not speaking of internal ructions within this or that party but within the broad area of Marxist theory. After all, theory must drive practice.

Marxism and the struggle for socialism must combine theory and practice. It is a given and almost a cliché. However, that most famous of quotes that 'theory without practice is sterile, practice without theory is blind' can never be a cliché. The fact that its truth becomes fudged and ignored is part of the reason that the left is in the state that it is and that capital is not being seriously challenged.

When theoreticians of Marxism become so caught up in posturing and in 'proving' to each other their particular vision and degree of cleverness, then the practitioners of Marxism face an unnecessary set of hurdles. It is hard enough to hold an ideology together in the face of a tsunami of bourgeois thought. To have the theory befogged by a thousand interpretations and a thousand claims to be the voice of Marxism in the 21st century, is to make life impossible. This is precisely what happened to the theory that was to change the world. It has become, for so many academic Marxists, something of a parlour game.

Now such a criticism may seem slightly away from the point of how theory is handled within a Marxist or Marxist-Leninist Party. This is probably true but the divergent trends in theory that today grow and multiply in the halls of academe are historically connected to the problems we see on the ground today and especially in the proliferation of political parties and organisations all claiming to be the 'one true church.'

The problem started before the 1917 Revolution. The rift between the ideas of reform or revolution tore the movement apart and breathed life into what has become a now decaying social democratic movement globally. The Revolution motivated working people the world over. Marxist-Leninist parties were formed off the back of that momentous event. It also wrought a crisis in the comfortable theorists' world. Marxism had become an almost exclusively European thing and especially a German thing. Quite soon after the Revolution, these anxious 'Marxist' thinkers found themselves in a quandary and quite torn. 'Do we support an eastward shift in the Marxist centre of gravity and away from Berlin, do we keep our theory safe but with no practice, or do we embrace a European expression of political thought in the form of social democracy?' With this dilemma was born the fragmentation of thought that resulted in the Frankfurt School, Western Marxism, and on to the New Left, and Eurocommunism and then via post-modernism to post-Marxist Marxism!

When a 'Marxist' theoretician can, with a straight face, state that the movement for socialism must avoid linking economic and political relationships, then we know we are in trouble. When we are told that a 'flaw' in Marxist analysis is its insistence that achieving socialism requires the working class to take power, then we can but wonder that so many communist parties are in such a poor state.

The organised left has had 'problems' with the working class for a long time. While capitalism was able to provide a reasonable standard of living and while the state was able to keep the working class in a fog of belief that their interests and those of the state are the same, then the work of communists has been doubly difficult. Many parties of the left have effectively left the field of battle, choosing instead to focus on the politics of identity or of 'broad' social movements. There have been enormous and astonishing contributions to the debate by the same academic Marxists to prove that this is the way to socialism.

This raises a question. If socialism is the end point and if a struggle against capitalism is the way to that end point, then what motivates people today to join a communist party? Is class still the dominant issue, or is it identity? The sincerity of the new recruit is undoubtedly there, but the theory of our movement is rooted in different soil. It is so clearly and obviously predicated on the working class, on the Party being the vanguard of the working class. Without such a lodestar, it is so much easier to be 'called away.' I cannot help but feel that a disregard of the working class, a retreat from the working class and an attempt to by-pass the working class for any identity-based movement is a departure from the theory of Marx, Engels and Lenin and a disregard for all those who have struggled for socialism and against capitalism.

Lenin famously derided those who were moving to the 'marsh' and showed that such a journey would end with nothing to show but leeches and wet feet. The problem with such a journey is that it is taken one small step at a time. Just as we read of the bushwalker who became hopelessly lost when he or she simply left the path for a minute to get a particularly good photo, so too do entire political parties become lost.

Parties espousing Marxism-Leninism as their core have always been prey to errors. Sometimes these have been of a left-sectarian nature and more frequently of a right opportunist leaning. Neither have any place within a Marxist-Leninist Party but either one or the other has all too often plagued the movement. Why? The answer is simple enough. The cadre force of the Party is all too often poorly educated in the ideology that forms the very soul of the Party and so if they do recognise the error, it is often too late.

A lot of time has been spent debating which departure from Marxism-Leninism is worse. As I, like so many before me, and sadly for those still to come, have been victims of these issues, and have brought them with us into the Party, or have learned them from others, it is worth just a few moments to consider the issue.

The question is often asked; which is the most destructive; Left or right opportunism? Leftism can have catastrophic consequences. Ultra-leftism and terrorism are the worst and most tragic manifestations of this trend. Isolation and self-satisfaction and a disdain for all but the party is another, albeit considerably less destructive tendency. Within the Marxist-Leninist Party things are generally less 'dramatic.' The party may shrink within itself. It might become doctrinaire and dogmatic; it might lose contact with the people. These are all negatives but rarely end in the liquidation of the party. It can recover. Right opportunism, on the other hand, diminishes the role of the party, hides its light under a bushel and often leads to a retreat from the essential purpose of the party and effectively, if unwittingly, weakens the party by focusing on building the 'movement', and unconsciously aligns itself with the logic of the revisionist Bernstein that 'it is the *journey* that is *important*, not the *destination*.' Things on the ground are often difficult. Winning the working class is difficult and so the role of the party can easily become subsumed into the broad social movements. It can and has led to a physical liquidation of the party.

A leading figure of the French Revolution of 1848, Alexandre Ledru-Rollin, is often cited as saying: 'there go the people. I must follow them, for I am their leader.' While the quote is unable to be verified and might well be apocryphal, the point is clear. It might be the call of any populist leader, from the right or the left. Communists need to be on guard against similar slurs, slanders, or even home truths that might be hurled against us. We must be on guard against accusations of 'tailism.' We must not lose sight of what we are for, why the party exists, and what are the objectives of the party. We must not step away from the historic mission of the communist movement for any brief 'sugar-hit' of this or that passing idea that deflects us from our purpose of working for the liberation of the working class. The lure of identity politics and the potential to engage, in order to simply show how 'progressive' our politics are, is strong, but does it challenge the rule of capital? If it does not, then it cannot be a defining or central focus for the party.

When politics become personal

I said a little earlier, and now repeat, that people join a communist party for all the right reasons. It is never for personal advancement, although the stroking of egos that go with small organisations, when one or two people assume 'power' and wield it happily, certainly can and does exist. But nobody would seek a life of ridiculously poor pay and conditions to work as a party functionary, if he or she were not committed. When the SPA was in the throes of a major split over the question of right opportunism in the Party, a journalist on the paper once joked that, 'of course I'm an opportunist. We will sweep into power any day now and then it'll be a life of chauffeured cars, beautiful women draped in furs, and a country house for me. Why else would I be here, balancing my broken desk leg with the phone book?'

No, people become communists because they see oppression, they see inequality, they see corruption and want a better world. They see war, climate destruction, they see racism and they want to do something about it. They see and they feel. Sometimes they 'feel' too much and too acutely. It is almost always an instinctual thing at first. You carry the anger with you. It sits with you alone and unshared. Then one day you might just come across someone with a newspaper, or a leaflet, or you find that book on a corner of a second-hand book stall and you no longer feel quite so desperately alone. There are others who share your thoughts and express them in a way that you have not yet consciously articulated.

That discovery, that there is a movement of people, just like yourself but seemingly so better qualified to give voice to your thoughts, is an important moment. The problem of whether or not this particular group has the right line, or appreciates the struggle, or understands Marxism, is at first secondary, but that can quickly become a problem, and a destructive one.

Today, in Australia there are at least 20 parties, groups and associations that have mutated from their original Trotskyist beginnings. There are five Parties proclaiming adherence to the mantle of Marxist-Leninist. The young, eager, well-meaning recruit to the cause, does not hold each of these parties up to any great scrutiny or analysis. There is no balance sheet by which to judge ideology, when you have no ideology and only an instinct to go by.

That choice, if it can in any sense be called a choice, is a decision often based on the person that draws you into the movement. Get it wrong and you can quickly become part of the flotsam and jetsam of former socialists that litter the political landscape.

If the party that you join deserves the title Marxist-Leninist, then you will and should have to jump through a few hoops before getting your party card. I remember, soon after first joining the SPA in Hobart having a conversation with a member of the old CPA. The SPA and the old CPA worked together on occasion, more by necessity than choice but then Hobart is a small place and home to a tiny left population. I sarcastically said to that CPA member that membership of the CPA was dependent on having a couple of dollars in your pocket at the right time. It was a cheap shot. He smiled and said that things needn't be as rigid as all that and that IOU's work out well. He was only half joking. Decades later I was witness to an Annual General Meeting of a branch of the CPA when Party cards were being issued. Only about one in seven members had paid their Pary dues. I couldn't help remembering that semi-serious, semi-joking conversation of 45 years earlier. It was with profound sadness that I asked myself; what have we come to?

Chapter Two

The stumbling path to the SPA

What have 'we' come to? Sitting here today, so soon after resigning from the CPA, ought to be a depressing moment. Paul Hogan's 'I'd give it away, if I were you' jibe to Frank Hardy ought to taunt me. It is neither a depressing decision and nor do Hogan's words have any meaning for me. What would be truly depressing would be to hang on to my Party card knowing that the Party has become something quite apart from the one I once joined. To cling to a hope that somehow it might be saved, that light might be shone into the dark recesses of the organisation, that it might once more stand as a proud Marxist-Leninist Party, and then recognise that this is but a dream and can never become reality would be depressing. To remain a member of a Party that is daily making a mockery, albeit unconsciously and unwittingly, of the lives of those thousands of courageous men and women who kept a flame of hope alive, who 'spurned the dust to win the prize', often sacrificing position, security, and health in their fight for the liberation of the working class, would be to sink into a slough of despond.

Leaving an organisation is not the same as deserting an idea. Communists live with and grow with a sense of revolutionary optimism. Our enemies might see that as being unrealistic; as simplistic, as naïve. So be it. The belief in the truth of Marxism-Leninism, coupled with the obvious terminal crisis in capitalism can only foster hope and confidence in the future. A party can go wrong. It can implode. But that is not the end of things.

Francis Fukuyama, at the time of the collapse of the Soviet Union, ridiculously wrote of the end of history. He seemed to believe that the world and capitalism would (now that socialism was out of the way and could do no more harm), move into a perpetual, harmonious, capitalist future. Since that prediction, capitalism has gone on to devastate the world and the working class. Everywhere working-class anger simmers. The global economy is on the edge of an abyss. Wars rage. The planet is threatened by climate change and global warming. The hands of the 'doomsday clock', set by the Bulletin of Atomic Scientists, have been reset at 89 seconds to midnight; the closest to global destruction since its inception in 1947 and the onset of the Cold War. Fukuyama's crystal ball let him down spectacularly. Reality was stronger than fantasy.

There has never been a greater need to challenge this reality. This 71-year-old communist knows that the future cannot be a continuation of the present. This gives me optimism.

My journey, first to the SPA and then back to the CPA so many years later, has been marked by occasional disappointments, and the odd defeat, but the objective necessity for change and for clarity in the movement against capitalism remains. The CPA has ceased, in my estimation, to be capable of playing any real part in effecting change, but the banner will not be permitted to lay in the dust. From degeneration and death comes regeneration and re-growth and re-birth. Of this I remain convinced.

There have been moments in my earlier life that can be seen, from the vantage point of time, to have been important. In retrospect they were signposts, roads taken or not taken, opportunities seized or missed. Chance can and does play a part, but I can only repeat what has already been said, that life is not merely chance. Something impels someone to make this or that turn. That something is, I suppose, the sum total of experiences, events, people, and inherent beliefs. The path, the trajectory of life can be a remarkable thing.

Childhood and childish views of the world

Children gain a worldview based on experience and importantly on what they are 'taught' by parents, teachers, and other voices that are deemed to be acceptable by the important adults around them. Hard and fast social attitudes are slowly inculcated. The mechanism of the capitalist state has worked diligently and without rest since capitalism and bourgeois ideology first emerged as the dominant idea. It has been enormously successful. It is almost impossible to think outside the square that this dominant ideology imposes. Marx once described how it took just two generations of ideological domination to make people believe that things had always been as they were; cruel, exploitative and unjust. A more recent permutation is that 'it is easier to imagine an end to the world than an end to capitalism.' Children learn quickly.

Part of this learning process is to learn to conform. Even so, children see injustice and unfairness and make protest to others. 'It's not fair.' Has any child not uttered that simple phrase. As they grow older, they tend to be 'knocked into shape.' An opinion formed in a child's mind based on an instinctive idea of justice, will be dismissed as being simplistic. They will be told that life is more complex. A process of conditioning is underway. Soon the 'simplistic' ideas are shelved and forgotten in favour of a comfortable *status quo*. Just occasionally, children slip through the net. Social conscience remains intact and the 'simplistic' remains a valued option.

When the child becomes an adult and still puts forward ideas that run counter to the prevailing attitudes, they are dismissed as either simplistic, dreamers, lacking in understanding of the complexities of life and the system or are simply written off as 'ratbags.' The communist, in an anti-communist world is the archetypal 'ratbag.' What the communist presents is truth. Sometimes the simple answer is the best and only answer worth listening to. There is inequality, poverty, exploitation. A better world is not only possible, or desirable, but must become a reality for the planet to survive. It is simple but true.

My childhood was in no sense different from those around me. I did, however, live in a slightly peculiar world that unconsciously allowed me to experience, almost in a laboratory setting, how society was ordered and how class ruled. I was, as a child, totally unaware of this. I had nothing to compare the village I grew up in. It was just my home, and my life. When my consciousness began to develop, that childhood helped rather than hindered me.

I was born in a village in the highlands of Tasmania. It was what was called a Hydro village. They were temporary places that were often temporary homes for the families of workers who built the dams and lakes and power stations that supplied hydroelectric power to the State. I spent the first 15 years of my life in two of these villages. The village was made up of about 200 prefabricated houses. They were set on stumps and simply relocated when the job finished. When the Hydro Schemes finally came to an end, attempts were made to sell these houses to poor urban or rather outer suburban homebuyers. No Council would permit it. The 'prefabs' were seen as substandard and unfit. We, who grew up in the villages were unaware of this, apart from the fact that they swayed rather interestingly in a strong wind. There was another, smaller group of houses. These were for a privileged group of specialist workers, designated 'staff.' They were not condemned and didn't sway in the wind. Slightly beyond the village was the 'camp.' Here lived about 800 single workers in huts and were fed from the Hydro camp kitchen. These workers came from European countries, and came in waves of migration; Greek, Italian. German, Spanish,

THE STUMBLING PATH TO THE SPA

Yugoslav. They put in a few years, saved money and moved on. There was also a contingent of Anglo-Australian workers who drifted in and out by turn. The single men were carefully segregated from the families. We would see them but never mix.

The migrant mix was also reflected in the enrolment at the local primary school. Each new group were mercilessly bullied until the next victims arrived.

The class divisions were amazingly well defined. There were ethnic divisions and inherent racism but everyone was ultimately in the same boat and everyone seemed to recognise this

None of this was an issue to a child in such a place. There was nothing to compare it with. Politics were a million miles from my life. The village and the one employer company town nature of this tiny village was intensely working class, although totally without of any semblance of class awareness let alone consciousness or any shadow of militancy. It's just how the employer, who was also landlord and primary shopkeeper in the village wanted it. My own family was no better or worse than anyone else's. My father was different from many of the men in town. He rarely drank, but he did gamble and with a passion. My parents had all of the prejudices of their generation but tried to imbue their sons with a sense of fair play. My father based his view of each passing wave of migrants on individual dealings. He had a good relationship with a couple of Yugoslavs and Italians and so, Yugoslavs and Italians were universally good and decent. He had a bad run in with one Greek. He harboured animosity towards Greeks until his dying day.

That is all a very long time ago. Did they encourage me? Did they offer support? As much or as little as any of my friends. Life went on without debates, without discussion, without books or ideas. I did not know anything different. Then, when I was about 15, we left the bush and moved to Hobart.

High school ended for me at the end of Grade 10. There was no money for the extra two years of school. So, I went to work. Ideas were flourishing and I first became vaguely aware that there were ideas beyond those of my parents. It was 1969 when I left school. By the end of another year, I had discovered the heady world of politics. Being at work, finding like-minded people in a political sense was, I believed, a liberating thing. I was, I thought, leaving childish things behind me.

An introduction to the 'left'

The first couple of years of the 1970s were exciting ones for me and politically formative ones. The Vietnam war was still raging. The protest movement had an impact on me. I went to the odd march and saw, in the lines of marchers, people who believed that they could stand against the apathy that surrounded them. These faces were not the subdued, empty faces of the people that looked back at me on the bus to work. Then something unexpected happened. I went, one Saturday or Sunday afternoon, to a concert in the grounds of the university. A young man was selling a left-wing newspaper. I bought a copy. The rest rapidly became history.

The paper was *Direct Action.* The organisation was the Socialist Youth Alliance. It seemed terribly important. There was almost a promise that huge changes were imminent. It was exciting. I got only a vague sense of the politics, but the paper talked about socialism, about how capitalism was the problem, that racism was a product of capitalism, that a better world was possible. As silly as it might sound nearly 55 years later, it was a cartoon that sealed the deal. A family, mum, dad, and two children were squeezed together on a couch, watching television; slack jawed and dull-eyed. The caption simply said, 'on the other hand you could be fanning the flames of discontent.' I made contact with the organisation and joined.

What followed was a round of meetings that often led to nothing, space on street corners was regularly occupied while attempting to sell the paper and achieving some small successes.

There were more meetings and often there was talk of the working class, although I can't remember anyone actually engaging with the working class. The nearest they had in Hobart to a worker was me. We were all little more than children but took ourselves very seriously. I assumed that things must be very different in the bigger cities. I found out a little later that this was not quite the case.

This 'worker' was employed as a clerk in an insurance office. I was asked to join my union and did. It was a small and very conservative union. Its Tasmaniuan president was also an executive member of the Liberal Party, and he worked in the same office as me. Still, I joined. This automatically made me the job delegate. An election was held, I was nominated and nobody stood against me. By some odd chance, or twist of fate I found myself a member of the State Executive of the union. The members of the union were happy enough to pay their dues but the idea of doing anything more was a bit of a joke, so the new boy was catapulted upwards.

My only claim to fame as a union delegate came when a strike was called by the Miscellaneous Workers' Union. Cleaners went out and other unions were urged to take solidarity action where possible. We were asked to help out by making sure that cleaning of the office stopped. Rubbish bins and waste-paper baskets were not be touched. The management of my workplace chose to defy this. The president of the union who worked at the next desk to me advised that we ignore the solidarity call. We were told to empty the bins. I rang the Misso's. The company had a black-ban imposed and I realised that my future as an insurance clerk was not looking all that great.

My time with the Socialist Youth Alliance was always going to be a short-lived one. The organisation morphed into the Socialist Workers' League and soon after it became known as the Socialist Workers' Party. It meanders along today as the Socialist Alliance.

My political education remained stunted. Nobody seemed much enamoured with the idea of political education. I still didn't know that it was really an essential requirement if you are to call yourself a socialist. I did learn how to manipulate meetings, white-ant other organisations to no particularly good purpose and some of the tactics that mark out the worst aspect of the politics of the Trotskyist movement. It seems that my belief that I had put childish things aside was not quite true.

The Vietnam war continued. Conscription was still an issue and the fact that I was rapidly approaching the date whereby I would have to register for national service was a dilemma for me. Would I or would I not register? The local Draft Resisters

Union was always on the lookout for a martyr and I was called, almost weekly, and urged to become a fugitive on their dubious behalf. In the end I didn't have to make the decision. 1972 ended with the election of Gough Whitlam. My dilemma went away.

Next steps along the road

I left the SYA. That didn't bother me unduly. I remained interested in the left, although there was no actual shape to anything. I moved from job to job and finally, more by luck than any sense of good judgement found my way back to school to finish my secondary education. I have the Whitlam government to thank for this. I was funded to go back under a 'retraining' scheme. By the end of that year – 1974 – I was eligible to enrol at one of the new Colleges of Advanced Education that had bobbed up across the country. The State government was spending money training teachers and so, with no real sense of vocation, I became a full-time undergraduate student-teacher.

The whole thing was a lucky break. I had been sacked from a job. Mass unemployment was just becoming a fact of life. I bumped into someone who suggested I go back to finish my schooling. The principal of the college (High schools in Tasmania finish at Year 10. Separate colleges complete the process) made it clear that I was welcome to study and that if I were to get a particular form filled in and back to the relevant government office, I could be paid to study. My former boss was reluctant to sign a declaration saying that I had been made redundant but eventually went along with the half-truth. All I had to do was complete the course, prove that I was psychologically sound enough to become a teacher, and then enrol for a four-year course that paid me near enough to a living wage, or at least allowed me to do the course and not do any part-time work to make ends meet. It was all a rather liberating experience. The only down-side to the deal was that I had to sign a bond to work as a teacher for at least two years.

By the time I became a full-time student-teacher, I had been out of politics for just two years. This, for organisations like the SYA which had in the interim been re-badged as the Socialist Workers' Party (SWP), is an eternity. I ran into the SWP at the College. Only one of my former comrades was still with them. Life expectancy in Trotskyist groups is very short. We had a sort of arms-length relationship for a time. But unexpectedly, my trajectory shifted dramatically soon after.

I had become involved in theatre. At an audition I met Rose Mazengarb. We spent a bit of time together as the play progressed. She was then what is best described as a 'fellow traveller' with the SWP. About three years later we married. Rose brought me back into the orbit of left politics. I helped the SWP on campus. I became involved in student politics but the relationship with the SWP was never a really close one and did not last long, although we bumped into each other for years to come and for the most part it was harmonious.

Rose and I, like so many before us and since, were looking for a political expression and a vehicle for that expression. Our search took us into the ALP in the late 1970s. It was an interesting period of my life. Politics hung in the air. The dismissal of the Whitlam government still rankled. The Fraser government offered something of a unity ticket for the left of all stripes, but our days in the Labor Party were marked by frustration and disappointment. We could find no home, no place of refuge in any of the factions within the ALP. Our politics were already beyond the official left faction of the Party. In Tasmania it was branded as the Broad Left. Broad it certainly was. Whether it was 'left' is another matter.

Something happened while this was beginning to affect us. In retrospect it was a life-changing 'something.'

We were invited to attend a meeting of the Australia-USSR Society. It was a casual invitation from another ALP member.

THE STUMBLING PATH TO THE SPA

It was a pleasant enough occasion and as ramshackle an affair as could be reasonably imagined. There was an odd mix in the room; a few ALP members, a couple of veteran communists who were later to become comrades, and an assortment of individuals who were there for all manner of reasons. There was a cheerful eccentricity to the group. We went away with an armful of magazines; some quite political and others not.

Time went by, but only a few months. We became involved with the Society and got to know the more political characters. Noel, the person who first got us involved, came to our place one evening with a question. Internationally, politics were taking an 'interesting' turn. The events in Afghanistan were rapidly coming to a head. He wanted to know what we thought and we shared a few ideas. He was as disillusioned with the ALP as we were. We began to meet to talk politics. He brought along a young friend of his. We invited the couple of veteran communists we had met as well and began reading *The Socialist*; the paper of the SPA.

Unbeknownst to us, one old ex-SPA member who was too frail to attend these ad-hoc discussions had decided that it was time to re-establish a branch of the Party in Hobart. We were asked to his house one afternoon, only to be confronted by a small group of people, most of whom we knew, as well as Jack

McPhillips, then National Organiser of the Party, whom I did not. He was there to sound us out quickly and just as quickly set the establishment of a branch in train. There was only one small difficulty in the plan. Nobody had thought to ask us what we thought about the grand plan. We were not ready for such a leap and were less than impressed about being railroaded. The meeting ended with McPhillips in high dudgeon. I later found out why. A Party Congress was in the offing. An extra branch would guarantee an extra two delegate votes and the Congress was going to be tight. We had no idea of the Machiavellian workings of the Party. That came a little later.

Our little group kept meeting and asked if we could have access to the pre-Congress discussion documents that were out for discussion with the Party. They came and we set to, reading, studying and discussing.

Joining the Party

One evening one of our discussion group said what each of us had been thinking but not saying. Why were we sitting here reading and talking? Why don't we join? About a month later Jack McPhillips made another visit to Hobart. We parted on better terms this time after he oversaw the branch formation and gave us our Parry cards.

The same old and frail ex-SPA member was ecstatic. He couldn't attend meetings but received his Party card. George Chenery was his name. He was one of those old-style working-class activists that grew with the Party over a lifetime. His house was lined with books and classical records. He had come to the old CPA as a young man. He was very young when he first came across class politics. He got to know some members of the International Workers of the World; the Wobblies. I remember him telling me how these men would wear white feathers in their laapels. They would go into pubs after work and knew they would have to face 'questions' about why they were not in uniform. Wearing the feather made discussion less time consuming. They did have to prove, from time to time that there is a difference between being a pacifist and being anti-war. Still, they were hard men and could more than hold their own.

Listening to these stories from George and from our two other older comrades, Alex and Lenny, gave me a feeling of continuity. We were part of one unbroken and unbreakable chain. As the Marxist left continues to embrace identity politics and shifts further and further from any real struggle with and for the working class, I feel that the great chain is weakening. All the more reason to fight for the future of the movement.

That feeling of continuity, of solidarity with those who had gone before us, strengthened our resolve. For me it was a feeling akin to coming home. This might sound a little sentimental or even theatrical, but that's how it was. The movement for socialism was local and it was international. It emboldened us all. Our older working-class comrades enlivened us. They had struggled against often terrible odds but knew that their fight was for their class. What they would make of so much of the poorly served Marxist movement and its adaptation to identity politics, to the politics of race and gender, to the politics of the quick-fix and to the ephemeral, I cannot say, but have more than a fair idea. At the same time, they were never narrow in their view. They championed all who needed championing, but they knew as Marxists, as Marxist-Leninists, as communists, that liberation comes from the defeat of capitalism and its state, and in the victory of the working class.

Those first weeks and months after joining the Party were a flurry of activity. We managed to pick up a few members and lost one or two along the way. It's never easy, swimming against the tide. Noel once commented that it was like selling something to someone who doesn't yet know they need what we offered. One of our first casualties was the young man who had urged us to join in the first place. The pull of career, family and the safety of the ALP was, ultimately greater than life in a small branch of the SPA. This is not an unusual story and can be understood. We parted on good terms. While living in Tasmania I bumped into him from time to time across the years. We are not close but we share a history, even if a brief history. We can meet without any awkwardness.

Another casualty was far more acrimonious. It was a case of expulsion after he refused to accept the direction of the branch and continued to go his own way after we had made the issue clear. The incident was public and in a public meeting. The whole branch was present when he broke ranks. The anger that the comrades felt was palpable. It was unpleasant but necessary. However, what marked out the branch and its membership was an extraordinary degree of comradeship. We were a diverse group but evolved in a very short time into a tight collective that cared for and about each other.

Hobart has always been a bit different, and no more so that when looking at the left, its make-up and the interactions between the groups. There was a branch of the old CPA. This was almost a 'ghost' branch in some ways. It existed. It remained invisible. It was a very comfortable club. The members had known each other for years and preferred not to frighten any horses. It had a presence in the Unemployed Workers' Union, but very little by way of a public face. It supported 'progressive' candidates in council elections and so on, but if you wanted to find any evidence of their presence, you had to go out of your way to dig for it. There was a tiny clutch of Maoists who focused entirely on the Australian Independence Movement. They ran an Independence stall at the local markets and kept themselves very much to themselves. Then there was the SWP who were going through a stage of entryism (sometimes spelled entrism and certainly pronounced that way) into the ALP.

Our arrival on the scene made life for the SWP difficult. They were tucked away in the ALP and we had a clear run, so to speak. We were busy. We sold a lot of papers, ran a market stall, were active in the Unemployed Workers' Union, set up an active peace organisation and re-activated the Friendship Society. On a clear night and when the wind was blowing in the right direction, you could almost hear the SWP grinding their collective teeth. We knew that they would have to come out. The ALP, if asked, would have been beastly careless.

Their entryism saw them ensconced in just one ALP branch. The ALP members around town used to cruelly refer to that branch as the 'Trot' branch. They were mildly useful to the

ALP, organising things, doing the donkey work and all the rest but it was just a couple of months after we emerged before they bounced back and onto the streets.

The left was small. Everyone knew everyone else. One memorable example was the night that the local art house cinema was screening a film that the left vigorously endorsed. By chance the entire organised left in Hobart all turned up on the same evening. To make it even more absurd, there was almost no-one else in the cinema. Each group distanced themselves physically from the others. It was all too much of a sad parody of Monty Python's *Life of Brian*.

While all of this was going on and we busied ourselves in and around the city we also, to the best of our rather limited abilities, addressed ourselves to theory. We ran classes on the basics of Marxism-Leninism; dialectical and historical materialism, economics and political history. The Party, at this time were pushing ideological education and we did the very best that we could.

The Party was in the process of splitting and as odd as it might seem to someone not there at the time, democratic centralism was smack bang in the middle of the stoush.

The dispute must have seemed to an outsider a bit like the Gulliver's Travels internal war between the big enders and the little enders and how best to take the top off a soft-boiled egg. It went, however, to a question of how dialectics was to be perceived.

The Party leadership argued that democratic centralism was a dialectical fusion of two opposing forces, thereby creating a new and distinct element. In this case there was, on one hand democracy and all it entailed, and on the other centralism and a formality and rigidity that went with it. Democratic centralism, under these terms becomes a melding of the two to create something new and distinct.

The opposing faction were guilty of running a right opportunist line which relegated the role of the Party to little more than an adjunct to the mass movement, and vigorously rejected this construction. They argued that democratic centralism was more akin to a line on a sliding scale with democracy at one pole and centralism at the other. Depending on the needs of the day, adjustments could be made; a bit more centralism or a bit more democracy. As I say, you really needed to have been there!

This was one of the debates that were to be fought out at the coming Party Congress. We were happy to accept the lead of the Party and, to be honest, had only the vaguest of ideas of the issue or of its coming importance. It did play a role in the branch and for the oddest of reasons.

We once had a pair of visiting 'lecturers' who surprisingly agreed to run a class on the question of democratic centralism. What made this so very odd was that the two 'lecturers' were not in town to talk theory to a Party branch. They were from the Soviet Embassy and under normal circumstances would never agree to even consider such an idea. But then again, Hobart was a bit different.

The Australia-USSR Society and other 'non-party' endeavours

We took an active part in the Society and had some success. It grew and prospered. Occasionally the Soviet Embassy would send someone down, or rather someone would do a bit of a national tour. Our part in this was to take the visitor around, hold the odd informal meeting with a sympathetic ALP politician, possibly get some minor media interest and, of course arrange a semi-public gathering under the auspices of the Society.

Two diplomats were coming to Hobart. They were to spend a few days in town. We set off to the airport to pick them up. On the way back we chanced our hand a bit and asked them if they might like to come to a Party meeting and especially if they would speak on what had become a most vexed question of democratic centralism. Protocol ought to have made this an impossibility but they seemed to be in something of an ebullient, holiday frame of mind. When asked, they said yes. They did as they were asked and we thought ourselves well served.

The rest of the visit went well enough, although remembered through a vodka haze. A public meeting had been arranged but our guests very nearly didn't get there. That had been taken away on a fishing excursion by a Russian émigré and dissident. The informal exercise in 'détente' was a success and given the high stake of intoxication of the guest speakers, the meeting was only partially embarrassing.

When waiting with them at the airport to catch their flight back to the security of the Embassy, they confided in us that the SPA was not the favoured organisation that it had once been. The split was well under way and the two diplomats let us know that the Communist Party of the Soviet Union were siding with our opposition faction. We sent this information off to Sydney. The Party leadership were not at all surprised, only that we had been told in quite so blunt a fashion by representatives of the Soviet Party.

THE STUMBLING PATH TO THE SPA

Naturally enough, our paths did not cross again. Soon after this event, one of the pair, Valery Ivanov was unceremoniously shown the door for spying.

Most of our time in the Society was far less exciting although we did believe that what we were doing was worthwhile and given the situation with the Cold War at its height and with anti-Soviet propaganda bubbling away, our efforts in a small way offered a hint of sanity and hoped to offer some balance to the worst of the anti-Soviet propaganda.

The Cold War and the real or perceived threat of war and nuclear war was also a time for peace and anti-war actions. The Party's primary slogan and one emblazoned on many of its banners was that we were 'the Party of Peace and Socialism.' At about the time we joined the SPA, the peace movement, nationally, took a major step forward. The United Nations had initiated a campaign for global nuclear disarmament and a global petition had been launched. The SPA set itself a task of getting many thousands of signatures and we, in Hobart took this challenge seriously. We had formed a branch of the Australian Peace Committee and through this organisation as well as efforts in the name of the Party, gathered well over a thousand signatures in rather quick time. This evolved into a period when the Palm Sunday Peace marches and rallies took shape around the country. These rallies became huge and hundreds of thousands of people across the country took part.

The Hobart branch of the Australian Peace Committee, managed to take a leading role within a group of peace activists and organisations. We assumed responsibility for the organisation of the first of these rallies. The rally was an outstanding success. We had speakers from Melbourne and Sydney and Rose acted as the MC and addressed the rally. We funded it from the proceeds of our market stall, selling nuts and nutbars. The nut business was rather an ingenious affair. A comrade in Melbourne was able to get stock at a ridiculously low price from a sympathetic wholesaler. They were then delivered to the wharves, where members of the seamen's union loaded them for shipment to Hobart. We would pick them up and one of our comrades would pack and weigh the nuts. As a result, we could sell very cheaply but still profitably.

Commitment and comrades

Our membership grew, but only very slowly. When we lamented this one of our older comrades, Alex, would repeat that numbers were less important than what we were and what we did. He was a remarkable man. He had cut his political teeth in London during the Depression, fighting 'Mosley's boys' as he described the British fascists. His politics grew from working in the Ford factory, meeting communists and attending meetings. Theory and practice came together when, as a young boxer, he discovered a group of young Jews who feared walking home after attending the gym. They were trying to learn how to defend themselves. Alex and a couple of his fellow boxers would see the Jews safely home. He soon joined the Party.

After the war he came to Australia and spent many years on the wharves. After retirement he took up the struggle for the unemployed. His politics were very sound and his capacity to 'cut to the chase' of an idea or argument was based on decades of practice. He applied himself to study and was especially pleased to be able to lead the branch in the occasional class. Life had dealt him a few rather difficult cards along the way but he remained infectiously optimistic about the struggle to which he had devoted his life.

Lenny was another remarkable communist in Hobart. He, too had been a wharfie in the hard times. When we got to know him, he had left the wharves and was working at the local brewery. His health had been destroyed by exposure to the elements.

He bitterly told us how the boss at the brewery had told the workers that a number would be retrenched. Lenny had perked up at this news. An early retirement was just what he needed and what his health demanded. The boss had smiled when he told him that he would be staying on. Lenny knew it was a punishment for his militancy on the job and his way of organising the workers.

Lenny was beloved in Hobart. Everyone knew him and there was barely a working-class family that he had not helped in one way or another. Thursday afternoon was the time that nobody, including management, ever interfered with him. He 'came by' large quantities of meat each week and Thursdays were given over to making up the orders for working class families across Hobart. He grudgingly allowed the boss to buy from him at the same ridiculously low price that everyone else paid. He was also a fine fund-raiser for the Party. He devised a sort of mini-lotto scheme which he called SPA-Lotto. He would sell tickets around the pubs. He was warned off at one point as the tickets needed to show that he had police permission. He brought his dilemma to the branch and asked if one of us could get a stamp made up with those magic words 'police permission.' It was done and he went on his way raising funds.

THE STUMBLING PATH TO THE SPA

These comrades, like so many over the decades were special people. They joined a struggle that was never going to be easy. They joined and they stayed the course. Many, myself included, take part in the journey for a time and leave. Some recommit, as we have done. Others are lost to the movement. Central to this problem has been an inability on the part of the Party to fully equip members with the ideological wherewithal to withstand the waves of bourgeois ideology that constantly crash over us all. When a truly committed, ideologically sound Marxist-Leninist Party is fully established, then I believe, the 'dead' will become fewer and the journey richer.

Our time in Hobart was intersected by the Fourth Party Congress and the split in the Party over the need to rid itself of a serious right opportunist error. The leadership of the SPA saw an opportunity to create a truly Marxist-Leninist Party, free from the lurching between sectarianism and opportunism. It fought for that goal but within a very short period of time opportunism re-asserted itself.

For Rose and I these were days that marked out our future, or at least the next part of our journey. Some months after becoming members of the SPA, Noel and I headed for Sydney and the Party Congress.

Chapter Three

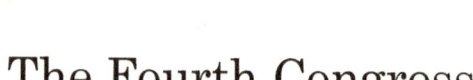

The Fourth Congress and commitment

Life changed for us when the Hobart branch of the SPA was formed. It also meant a fairly dramatic change of pace for me. None of us were really ready for this. We were building something from scratch. According to the Party rules and Constitution new recruits were to be carefully brought into the life of the branch and the Party. We had nobody to mentor us. We had to do it all ourselves. I was chosen to be branch secretary. Looking back, I believe that we did a pretty good job.

Despite our lack of experience and despite the lack of any guiding hand, we threw ourselves into the fray. We took our Party responsibilities very seriously and possibly more so because of our isolation from the centre of political action in Sydney. These were the days before cheap airline tickets. There were no frequent flyer points to be clocked up. A trip to Sydney was not to be entered into lightly and comrades from the centre were infrequent flyers. So, when we heard that this or that was to be seen as important, then we responded.

We read, in our paper, *The Socialist*, and had heard Jack McPhillips say that the paper was the lungs of the Party. We accepted this and accepted the importance of distributing the paper as widely as possible. All Party members were exhorted to sell it, write for it and send ideas for stories on a regular basis. None of us had any experience in journalism or in any form of writing, but needs must. It seemed logical, or that was how it was pitched, that the branch secretary ought to shoulder that responsibility. A large box containing various books, pamphlets and magazines that constituted the 'library' and archive of the Australia-USSR Society was given to Rose and me for safe-keeping. There was also a type-writer, the like of which had not been seen for decades. It was from the German Democratic Republic. Fortunately, I was young enough and sound of limb because it needed some strength to lift the machine. It was clearly built to last.

We had nowhere to put it so it sat in all its glory on top of a chest of drawers in our bedroom. I had to stand to use it and never having typed anything before, spent a good deal of time bashing away at the keyboard. Articles were first laboriously hand-written and then typed before sending. To be honest the quantity of material sent was rather sporadic, and the quality was hardly inspiring but a beginning had been made.

The aged, but not terribly infirm machine, also produced reports for the branch and soon, I wrote my first tentative articles around the coming split. I was encouraged to write about the bubbling inner-Party dispute, although if truth be told I was rather out of my depth. My grip on theory was hardly up to scratch. When I look at what has become of the now CPA and the dismal level of political awareness and lack of theoretical development, we didn't do too badly, although that is of little comfort.

Among the dusty and little-used books in the USSR Society's Big Box was a little red-covered book of quotes. They were primarily from Lenin, but also had a goodly smattering from Marx and Engels. The really useful thing was that they were grouped around themes and dealt with debates and disputes in the Marxist movement in Russia before and at the time of the Revolution. When one of our opponents in the on-going round of polemics between the Party and the right opportunists would fire off a barb, it would be quickly responded to. Armed with this little 'cheat sheet' of a book, I took up arms. It was easy, although any scholar of the movement would dismiss my work as 'derivative' and they would be absolutely correct. I would find an appropriate number of quotes to support 'our' position and link them with brief paragraphs or simply the odd sentence. It didn't mean that I knew what I was talking about but my sources did, and after all, if it was good enough for Marx, Engels and Lenin, then surely that was enough.

Semi-consciously and stumblingly, I was beginning to pick up a few useful skills. My late brother-in-law, David Mazengarb, a one-time member of the SWP often spoke of the debt we all owe to our membership of parties such as ours for developing skills we might never have discovered. We learned how to write, produce leaflets, speak, research (in a limited way), handle the media, organise, raise funds and appear to be confident in doing all of this.

We are watching history comrade

We had been active in the Party for only a few months when the Fourth Party Congress opened in October 1981. It seemed that our preparation for membership and our activism in the branch was also geared toward these few days.

A Party Congress, held every three or sometimes four years is a gathering of delegates from across the country. It is the culmination of a lengthy period of discussion within branches of a major document, the Political Resolution that guides the work of the Party until the next Congress. It might also amend the Program of the Party or the Constitution, if required. It elects a new Central Committee that guides the work of the Party, which in turn elects higher committees.

The Congress therefore is a culmination of intense internal political discussion. If there are problems, it is during this period that they will emerge. If they cannot be resolved, then the Congress can become an arena for furious ideological battle, and political blood-letting. It was into this arena that the two observers from Hobart, myself and Noel Miley found themselves. We were not voting delegates. Our branch had been constituted just outside the deadline. This still rankled with the Party Organiser, Jack McPhillips who was counting delegates and votes with intensity. As I recall, there were about 100 delegates. The voting split was 52-48 or thereabouts. The difference might have been as close as two votes.

There were two distinct and clearly identified factions, although factionalism was prohibited in the Party. Both were clothed in a high degree of ideological garb. Both used theory

THE FOURTH CONGRESS AND COMMITMENT

and theoretical arguments to prove that they were right. Both had forceful advocates and these comrades had decades of experience to draw upon. Both sides had followers. What we saw in the few days of battle was just how seriously did each side take the struggle. The gloves were off.

The Party leadership; the General-Secretary, Peter Symon and the National Organiser, Jack McPhillips occupied one corner in this battle. In the other corner was the Party President, Pat Clancy and a leading figure in the mass, non-party organisations and theoretician, Bill Brown.

The power base for the Symon-McPhillips group was in the Party Centre, in the paper, the growing youth group and in newly formed and burgeoning locality branches in Sydney. They also had the broad support of the migrant branches and in other States.

The Clancy-Brown forces were based in some of the more powerful trade unions in the country and especially in the Building Workers' Industrial Union, which later became a significant element in the CFMEU, the Seamen's Union, Miner's, and sections of the Waterside Workers' Union They also had the support of the Soviet-affiliated Women's, Peace and Youth organisations.

In the briefest of terms, the debate was whether one side was right opportunist which they strongly refuted, or that the other side was left sectarian, which was equally and loudly argued against. The rift was deep. It was deeper than simply a struggle about who would control and lead the Party. It was about what sort of Party was needed in Australia and how to go about building it.

What was important in all this was that we were witnessing a struggle between forces with a collective membership and commitment to the communist movement spanning many decades. It was a struggle that shaped the future of the Marxist-Leninist movement in Australia. This might seem melodramatic, especially when we can look at the paucity of ideas that exist in the CPA today, of the dismal level of ideological capacity, and when party education is nominal at the very best.

The Party had in the very few years since its formation from the split in the old CPA grown substantially. Hundreds of younger members had joined. There were large numbers of new members who had come from the migrant communities; Lebanese, Turkish, Greek, among others. There were large numbers of industrial members; building workers, miners, wharfies, and seamen. The assembled delegates represented these groups. We watched, listened and were impressed.

THE FOURTH CONGRESS AND COMMITMENT

Never having experienced a gathering such as this, I was unaware of its importance. Naturally I had the sense that what was unfolding was not a usual occurrence. I had been made aware that a struggle was underway, but just the same, the life and death nature of it became intoxicating. But even so, I could not know just how different it was from any 'normal' national meeting. The heat, the intensity of things became apparent when a Sydney comrade we had only just met, slipped into a vacant chair next to us and said quietly, while keeping his eyes fixed on the speaker's podium, that 'we are watching history, comrades.'

In time we came to know this comrade well. Eddie Clynes was one of those who devoted his life to the Party, working for many years as a full-time functionary. Sadly, he died long before his time.

But when Eddie made that remark, I wondered at what seemed to be an exaggerated expression, but as private discussions continued and the debates went on, it was impossible not to feel that the stakes were high. To the victor go the spoils. The Party had been experiencing a significant growth spurt. It was just a decade since it had come into being after the old CPA expelled some members and others resigned. History, such as it has been recorded, puts that split down to differences relating to the USSR. This was undoubtedly a strong factor, but as in all ruptures in the communist movement, there were deep ideological issues that simply could not be resolved.

The old CPA had adopted what was called Eurocommunism as a theoretical perspective. Those about to leave or be expelled saw this trend in the world movement as a step towards a social democratic position and closely akin to debates fought out in the earliest years of the 20th century when social democracy and Marxism irrevocably split.

History has a habit of revisiting the Marxist movement. When the split in the old CPA came about, few gave much hope for the new party. The SPA was small. Its membership was older. Their resources were few and yet within a very small period of time the Party grew into a vibrant organisation with branches across the country, with a growing youth organisation and with a renewed desire to study. All of this should have augured well but even as many branches were busy recruiting new members, and studying Marxist-Leninist theory, it was by no means conducted fully, particularly well and by no means evenly or across all sections of the Party.

Life for a communist in a country so bound by bourgeois thought and ideology is never easy. The ideology of capitalism, of bourgeois democracy, of the philosophy that guides society and guards against change, seeps into your very pores; so easily

THE FOURTH CONGRESS AND COMMITMENT

and without leaving any trace. It is always so simple to take a wrong step, misread this or that signal, to seek support in other organisations, to place emphasis on building a mass movement while ignoring the role of the party. This is a sad reflection, not simply of Australian political reality, bur across all continents and can afflict and affect any party at any time. The tendency is to drift to the right, to right opportunism. A 'correction' is sometimes made and the opposite error, of left sectarianism comes to the fore. It was once asked, which error is the worst? The answer came; the one you are not fighting. While the SPA leadership recognised this, and fought for a Party that might grow without such ideological wobbling, the sad truth is that probably less than a decade later, the error that was no longer being fought began to reassert itself and has, today all but destroyed the Party. A communist party must be a party of activists but it must be guided by theory. Getting the theoretical structure right is so very important. Neglect leads to political death.

The Fourth Congress was about just such a fight, but was more than just another inner-party blood-letting. There was a concerted effort to fight the right opportunists without sliding into a left sectarian morass. This was, of course, easier said than done but such was the intent and that is what made that comrade say to us that we were sitting and watching history being made. It was not an exaggeration and nor was it melodramatic in the slightest. Whether or not the Party had the ideological armour to not simply win a Congress but to forge a party strong enough for the tasks it was setting itself was quite another matter.

The aftermath

After three days of relentless combat, the Congress came to a close. The changes to the Party Program were passed. The Political Resolution was adopted. There were victors and there were vanquished. But things are never quite as neat as all that and nothing was ever quite the same.

The fallout was almost immediate. The bulk of resignations came a bit later. Clancy did not formally leave the SPA until 1983, but everyone knew where everyone stood. Bill Brown and Pat Clancy moved relatively quickly to form the Association for Communist Unity (ACU) in 1984. It was presented as an attempt at reuniting the left. It had a brief moment in the sun. As far as 'reuniting' the movement, it was an abject failure. It attracted the dissident forces who had left the SPA. This was a grouping that included the leadership of the BWIU, the Seamen's Union of Australia (SUA), sections of the Waterside Worker's Federation, and others. On paper it looked formidable enough. At the time of the Congress, the Building branch in Sydney had over 80 members. There were 1,000 members of the SUA and 100 of the total membership carried a SPA Pary card. However, Peter Symon said, repeatedly, 'a party will need functionaries. It will need a paper. It will need a cadre-force prepared to do the work. He was right. He spoke from experience. The functionaries of the SPA continued a long tradition of sacrifice and for foolishly low wages. When the SPA was formed, Bill Brown had been asked to edit the new Party paper. He had in an earlier life worked as a full-time journalist on a Sydney bourgeois newspaper. He refused to take the job, explaining that he wanted to be free to pursue a range of activities. The ACU did produce a journal. It appeared for a time. It ceased publication and the ACU slipped below the waves.

Although the losses in membership ought to have dealt a major blow to the Party, it was not immediately evident. Work went on. We, in the SPA, were vindicated in our assessment of what had become known as the Clancy-Brown forces. In 1983, Bob Hawke became Prime Minister. Neoliberalist economics was sweeping the world as the system sought ways to stave off the crisis that was tearing through the world capitalist economy. 'Reaganomics' and Thatcherism arrived in Australia in the guise of the ALP and social democracy.

Theory and practice are tested in day-to-day life and struggle. The assessment that the SPA had of the political trajectory of those designated as right opportunist was almost immediately tested. The correctness of that assessment and the line adopted by the Party hit home very soon after the coming to power of Hawke and Keating in 1983. The infamous Accord between government, business and unions included among its authors, Laurie Carmichael, then a prominent member of the old CPA and Tom McDonald. McDonald was a leader of the BWIU and, along with his mentor Pat Clancy and Bill Brown, a leading figure in the deposed faction in the SPA.

The ramifications of this document far outlived its time as policy. It was denounced by the Party as class collaborationist. This was obviously the case. The shackling of the unions, the dramatic decline in membership, the abandonment of any pretence at defending workers' rights, can all be directly traced back to that document; a document signed by alleged communist union officials and members of parties claiming adherence to Marx, Engels, Lenin and class struggle.

The Accord and the right-ward drift of the ex-SPA forces all occurred while Rose and I were out of the country. We had been sent to Moscow by the Party and spent three years there. They were tumultuous years, personally, and politically; both within the Soviet Union and in the SPA. Our path to Moscow came, not immediately after the fourth Congress but within the shadow of that historic gathering. The better part of a year elapsed before we boarded the plane for Moscow.

Final months in Hobart

Noel Miley and I returned to Hobart after the Congress. Our reports to the branch were positive ones. We were able to speak of the intensity of political activity across the country and of the way the political debates played out.

Our small branch suffered from geographic isolation. It did us all good to know that, despite the negative nature of the looming split, things were really quite healthy. The Young Socialist League (YSL) was doing well, and winning people to our cause. It was consciously building cadres for the Party. The strength of the Party in the Arabic community and among Greek and Cypriot communities was impressive. The fragmenting of the peace movement, and therefore weakening of the Australian Peace Committee, was yet to be felt. The same went for the

Union of Australian Women. But even as clouds were gathering, there was a sense of unity of purpose and optimism among us.

Reports of the inner-Party struggle were absorbed with a sense of sadness as well as an understanding that our struggle was bigger than personalities. Our comrades in Hobart, as in all branches across the country, knew and understood the importance of the issues at stake. As far as any loss of membership was concerned, this was summed up in the perpetually optimistic words of Alex Randall. One of his favourite sayings was that 'one communist is worth fifty social democrats.' He quickly adapted that to include those who accommodated themselves too eagerly to the politics of social democracy. He was also fond of saying that our greatest weapon was patience. 'We've got time on our side.' Time! Alex never saw his life-time's work come to anything like fruition but he knew what he was talking about. History rolls on. An absolute of Marxist theory is historical materialism and that change will come and must come. Entire social and economic formations come, control, appear to be immutable, and pass away. We, as individuals do not, cannot compel the tide to turn back and nor can we issue declarations that change will come at our will or to meet a preferred deadline. The Alex's, the Lenny's of my acquaintance, the hundreds and thousands of brave men and women who have gone before knew that the Revolution was not imminent but nevertheless fought with tenacity for that future.

They knew that history while moving inexorably forward does not always travel in a straight line. The news that the Party was in the throes of a split and that men and women whose names were linked to a shared past, would soon leave us, was but a brief concern. The Party was what counted and it counted because it stood for something worth fighting for.

And so, our work continued. We met, we discussed, we sold papers, we ran a stall at the market, we engaged in mass work when and where possible, we engaged in solidarity with other groups when appropriate. We worked.

Sometimes our efforts were rewarded and sometimes we hit walls and suffered setbacks. We formed a branch of the Australian Peace Committee (APC) and sought to incorporate other peace groups under its banner. We met with hostility as some less than supportive souls denounced the APC as a Soviet front organisation. It all came to a head at a heated and doomed meeting that was to vote on acceptance of the APC or not. We stuck to our guns. We clung to the idea of principle. A radical priest was chairing the meeting. Before it opened, he called a couple of us aside and urged us to delay the vote as our opponents had been caucusing rather effectively and a clear stacking of the meeting was underway. We ignored his advice. One of the more virulent speakers against us that evening was a member of the SPA! He chose to break with Party discipline and go his own way, in the hope that he would rise to the top of the rival group. His cards were marked. He was expelled from the SPA and was quickly rejected by the other factions in the peace movement. Living by the sword so often ends badly. He did lay counter-charges against me as the branch secretary. We were told about this a little later by comrades in Sydney who ignored the affair.

Two peace groups vied with each other briefly. It was against this period of hostility in the name of peace that we pledged to fund the first of the major Palm Sunday rallies in Hobart. The figurative swords were not entirely turned into ploughshares but at least the blades returned to their sheathes.

The left in Hobart usually managed to rub along or almost always. There were times when animosity overwhelmed good sense. One issue that both united and divided the left in Hobart was the work of the Unemployed Worker's Union (UWU) Alex had been an activist with the UWU at the time of the birth of the SPA branch. He was responsible, along with an ex-seaman in Hobart, for setting up the popular and profitable nut business. The old CPA managed to rouse themselves from their torpor and moved people into the UWU. There was a building, resources and although precious few unemployed workers ever crossed the threshold, it offered the CPA a sense of legitimacy.

The CPA and SPA members involved in this area of work were cordial enough, although the CPA were not entirely welcoming. One seemingly harmless initiative led rapidly to a falling out and the withdrawal of the SPA from the UWU. Someone suggested that as the union building was being used as a bit of a drop-in centre and meeting space as well as a shop-front, it would be a good idea to sell a few books. Rose and a woman from the CPA sorted this out and an incredibly short-lived 'left bookshelf' opened. It was literally a shelf. On one side was a selection of our books and on the other sat some CPA titles. Sales were predictably low but that mattered little. One morning Rose and Alex arrived at the shop to discover that several of our books had miraculously 'fallen' into a rubbish bin placed at the SPA end of the shelf. War was almost declared. Alex erupted.

Providing for the nut stall, the shop and the stock was all down to his labour. He let us know that his labour was being withdrawn. I went to see my CPA counterpart to give him the news that all bets were off. The CPA kept the office and shop. We kept the market stall.

Some time later while Rose and I were in Moscow, the ill-fated UWU building became the source of a takeover by the SWP, and then after they had turned it into a profit-making venture, their comrades in Melbourne rolled the Hobart branch to get at the loot. It was all very grubby.

A Tasmanian 'exceptionalism'

Hobart has traditionally been a graveyard for the left. Groups have come, formed, recruited and disintegrated. The bigger political centres for these parties have sometimes pulled people out of Hobart to strengthen other branches. Sometimes people have been sent to Hobart to build branches. This had always been the strategy of the SWP. It invariably ended badly. The cadre that was sent to Hobart often left the Party. Cynical voices like Jack McPhillips were heard to say that whatever cables connected it to the rest of the country should be severed completely, the island towed toward the Antarctic and either forgotten about or sunk. An SWP figure used to say that after the Revolution, Tasmania would be kept as a museum because nothing ever changed anyway.

THE FOURTH CONGRESS AND COMMITMENT

The problem for the left was that there had never been anything like an industrial working class in any numbers. The working class is, at best, difficult to organise into class-conscious workers. That has been one of the reasons that 'academic' Marxist theoreticians that grew around the Frankfurt School, Western Marxism and later the New Left felt compelled to 'rescue' Marxism. In particular the period after WWII saw a growing acquiescence among the working class. Capitalism appeared to have righted itself and the 'golden age' of capitalism from the end of the war until the early 1970sw saw real wages rise, working conditions improve and many theorists began to believe the arguments that capitalism was a self-regulating system and not prone to collapse as Marx contended. Bernstein seemed to be, at last, in the ascendancy.

This trend in Marxism led to a steep descent into opportunism. The most obvious manifestation of it in the world Marxist movement was in the form of Eurocommunism, which had more to do with social democratic thinking that to Marxism-Leninism. The old CPA was a casualty of this philosophy. The current CPA might refuse to see it, but they have adapted themselves to this same ideological perspective.

We, in Hobart, were unaware of any of that. We had little real contact with the working class. We contented ourselves with working with what was before us. The position of the working class in Tasmania was rather different from what could be seen in other States. Prior to WWII the Tasmanian economy had been primarily an agricultural one. This began to change in the post-war period, thanks largely to the development of massive hydroelectric schemes. The Hydro Electric Commission (HEC) was charged with producing cheap electricity that would draw big industries to the island and secure an economic future. There were a couple of successes but 30 per cent of the total State budget was consumed by the HEC to very little avail. It did mean a constant revolve of immigrant workers who came, sometimes stayed and but more often moved on. These workers lived in isolated camps far from the urban centres and were motivated by the desire to get in, make a quick killing, and get out.

The electrification of the island combined with the limited industrialisation did shift the demographics a little. There was less reliance on agriculture but the new working class grew as the 'golden age' of capitalism grew. Industrial actions were few and far between. Apart from a short, three-year period from 1969-72, the right-wing dominated ALP ruled continuously for 48 years from 1934 until 1982. The working class were among the least politicised sections of the population. When in the early 1980s the dramatic anti-dam movement erupted, the beneficiary, politically, was the Liberal Party who won the working-class vote.

The left toiled in this arid soil but with little success. As a consequence, and unconsciously, the left and by implication the SPA in Hobart remained separate from the working class. The bulk of our work was in and among the middle class. This did not mean that we did not recognise the importance of building the Party and extending its influence and visibility among the working class. Tasmania, under the decades-long domination of the ALP, had invested heavily in public housing. The State was perennially on the brink of economic recession and the post-war welfare-statist policies in the West were reflected in Tasmania. Public housing projects began in areas relatively close to the city but increasingly large 'greenfield' developments were built on the very edge of Hobart. They were soulless places, devoid of trees or any green spaces, lacked facilities, and had limited access to public transport. Poverty was entrenched and intergenerational.

Two of our comrades, a husband-and-wife team lived in one of these Housing Commission suburbs; Bridgewater-Gagebrook. He had been elected to the Hobart City Council before joining the SPA. He also ran a small local newspaper. Under his guidance, the branch did some work in the area. It was a time of economic downturn and this affected an already impoverished community badly. Evictions were being carried out. The State was the landlord. The ALP was in power. We spoke at local meetings, talked to people, distributed the paper and leaflets, but were seen as possibly too 'exotic.' There was no history of action in these devastated communities.

Before joining the Party, Brian Smith, the Councillor, had considered packing his family up and emigrating to the USSR. George Chenery, an aged and infirm comrade, rallied his strength and railed against this behaviour. To comrade George it was a case of don't be so foolish or selfish. In very unsubtle tones he pointed out that socialism needed to be fought for here and now. Brian was suitably chastised about wanting to jump ship in order to 'lap up their system.'

At about the same time that Brian was being berated, a local ALP stalwart, leading member of the Australia-USSR society and peace activist, George Shenman was complaining that he was 'sick of it' and half in jest said he might emigrate to the Soviet Union. Chenery was not a confidante of Shenman and was saved from repeating the dose.

George and Doreen Shenman were staunch supporters of the USSR although would never, could never, leave the ALP.

They remained critical of it but accepted their life membership with pride. I well remember sitting in their living room and looking at a framed photo on the wall. They explained it to Rose and me. It was a picture of the Central Committee of the Bolshevik Party and was taken almost immediately after the Revolution. George's father was in the picture. George and Doreen were equally proud of the connection, and for good reason. George was born in the early 1920's and he spent part of his babyhood in a creche set up in the Kremlin. His father was an economist and was sent to the UK just a few years before Stalin's early purges. The Sheinman family stayed in England, slightly anglicised the name and never went back home.

While we were in Moscow, George and Doreen visited. They holidayed for a time while George waited to begin an advanced Russian language course. He stayed on for some months. A veterinarian surgeon by profession, he later came to use his Russian as a translator in Hobart.

Getting the call to Moscow

While our work in Hobart continued, my typing skills improved marginally. The veteran GDR typewriter and I were building a relationship of sorts. Rose and I had a couple of short visits to

Sydney where we met with and had talks with some of the leading cadre in the Party. We were confirmed in our view that they were on the right track and so it followed must we.

Back in Hobart I wrote my first stumbling article for the Party's theoretical journal the *Australian Marxist Review*. I was reluctant to do so but was urged on by Peter Symon. I felt tentative about it, but I took my role seriously and was not about to say no.

We heard that Jack McPhillips was doing something like a tour of branches and was due in Hobart. We went through our usual paces and then he asked what appeared to be a casual sort of question. Would we like to go to Moscow and would I like to take up a job as correspondent for the paper. It was such an unlikely question. We answered yes without thought. In our mind it was almost in the realm of fantasy. It was not that far removed from 'what would you do if you won the lotto' or 'choose any city in the world to live for a year.' Jack's question was, in our estimation, almost as fanciful. He said no more about it, but when leaving he made an oblique reference to talking further about Moscow.

Obviously Rose and I talked about all this but it wasn't for a little while that it took on more serious and tangible shape. It was Peter Symon who made the proposition a formal thing. The

THE FOURTH CONGRESS AND COMMITMENT

plan was for us to go for two years. As it turned out the two years turned into three. Our resident in Moscow at the time was Jim Mitchell who was wanting to come home to Adelaide to a sort of retirement. The arrangements would take some time. It was only, little by little, that the hidden difficulties associated with the task were made clear to us.

We were young, inexperienced, relatively new recruits and yet were about to be sent to the epicentre of the world communist movement. We got wind, fairly quickly that at least a couple of noses were just a little out of joint. One South Australian comrade in particular was rather peeved by the decision. Rose was to join a student group that was leaving Australia at about the time we were due to leave. The group was to spend 12 months at what was simply called the Party school or the Lenin school. We had no personal knowledge of these comrades apart from a casual meeting with a married couple from Sydney. This student group and their fortunes in the USSR was to became significant.

My job was seemingly straight-forward enough, at least that's how it appeared from the safety and security of our fireside in North Hobart. I would write materials for the paper, represent the Party in a limited form and we would act as something of a cross between a pair of jovial mine-hosts to visiting comrades and fellow travellers, and as unofficial Australian communist ambassadors. What could possibly go wrong? After all the SPA and the CPSU had fraternal relations. We were just the latest in a line of similar appointments stretching way back. All would be rosy, or at least that was how our naïve estimation of things ran.

We waited but didn't break the news to our comrades. After all nothing is ever set in concrete. Finally, the confirmation phone call came. Even so, there could be no fixed departure date as visas and the rest took an interminable time. The following weeks were busy ones. The branch members were both pleased and a little put out. We were a small group. Taking two people out was obviously going to be tricky. Still, plans were made, and the branch managed without us for a few years more. There were a few touchy moments with my family, or at least my two brothers, or to be even more precise, their wives who seemed to take the news as something of a personal affront. This had little effect on us as our paths had diverged long ago. Rose's family were far less critical. One brother was a member of the SWP. He just wrote it off to our political 'failings' but had always had a special relationship with Rose. Another brother was in the army. He was untouched by any of it and embraced the idea of the adventure warmly. A third brother was a little perplexed as he couldn't fathom why we ever broke from the ALP. Families are funny things.

The time finally arrived. A young comrade took over the lease on our house. We sold off as much as we could and stored what we thought we needed for the future under another comrade's house. I left my job, and we headed to Sydney for a final briefing and then, away.

It won't be easy

The final few days before leaving were spent in Sydney. It was here that we met two comrades, Peter and Donna McLaren. They lived in a tiny place in Petersham, but managed somehow to squeeze us in for a couple of nights. It was a squeeze as our two children accompanied us. Forty-four years later, I had the very good fortune to meet Peter once more. By the time we met again, I had spent many years outside the Party but had re-joined. After 18 months I was beginning to seriously question that decision. The Party was not even a rump of its former self and that is possibly being kind. It bears no relation to the one that we joined all those years ago. Peter gave me hope. He had remained steadfast to his beliefs. He is a Marxist-Leninist. And because he is a communist, he walked away from the CPA.

He, and a number of other veterans of the struggle recognised that to remain in such a Party was destructive. They are now a part of a new Marxist-Leninist political organisation that offers hope.

Forty-four years is a long time. Much happens in that time. So many stops and starts, halts and beginnings. So many mistakes, so many attempts to right wrongs, and so much handy hindsight. But, in September 1982, our sights were set on the future and not the past. We arrived in Sydney, suitcases bulging, but ever-so-carefully not overweight. The days leading up to departure were spent locked in a series of meetings with central leadership cadres and especially with Peter Symon. These meetings were held in private, away from prying ears.

The Soviet Party, we were told, had made no bones about its support for Pat Clancy, Bill Brown and their faction. Rose and I were seen to have less political 'baggage.' Our relatively new status was seen as an advantage, but we were warned that things would not be easy in our dealings with the Soviet comrades and in particular the International Department and its representative who was responsible for our part of the world. Symon sought to reassure us that all the necessary protocols would be observed and that our work would not be impeded but that we needed to be aware of things and to not be surprised at any reluctance on their part to go out of their way for us.

He also outlined just how deep the relationship, both personal and ideological, ran between the CPSU and Clancy. Pat Clancy's position in the trade union movement gave him the ear of government. He liked to tell people that Bob Hawke often consulted with him. This influence in the eyes of the CPSU was important, or at least gave the appearance of great importance. The opportunist faction controlled significant union positions and mass, non-party organisations that were being used to foster better relations between Australia and the Soviet Union. This level of political opportunism suited the CPSU rather well. They were less inclined to support the SPA in its struggle to build itself as a firm Marxist-Leninist Party.

We were exhorted to be firm, to act in the best interests of the Parry, to maintain positive relations with our hosts and 'suffer the slings and arrows of outrageous fortune.' It was all a bit daunting but there was no turning back. We gave our word that we could be trusted and that we would not let anyone down.

Rose and I, in the moments we had in private, mulled on all this. We knew that things would not be a bed of roses. We had a deep faith in the Party and the Soviet Union. Surely these were not all that contradictory. As it turned out the reception that we received was cordial but the day-to-day workings became more and more perfunctory. We were possibly naïve, undoubtedly idealistic, but possibly this acted in our favour. We remained doggedly true to our colours and our pledge not to let anyone down.

We were ultimately ferried to the airport and farewells were made. First stop Singapore and then a change of plane and our first introduction, via Aeroflot, to the Soviet Union.

The flight from Singapore to Moscow was, and is still, a long one. There was a brief and intensely uncomfortable refuelling stop in India before the final leg of the journey. Aeroflot Airlines was, I suppose, minimalist in form. The plane was no better or worse than most. The cabin crew were quite different and it was a difference that charmed us. The crew did their job efficiently but with no sense of servility. Civil but not servile. It was an attitude that became normal for us but at that very moment struck us as being different.

Chapter Four

And so, to the Soviet Union

It was just after dawn that our flight touched down at Scheremetyevo airport. It was misty but we had caught our first sight of the Soviet Union. We were greeted on the plane by Valery Koudinov. He was our contact in the International Department. We four weary travellers followed him down the stairs and onto a very cold tarmac and then into the terminal. The temperature was minus one degree. It was still autumn. Winter clothes would have to be a priority.

We were ushered into a lounge area before heading off to our new home. One of the perks of the job was that we did not have to go through customs. Our passports remained unstamped. It wasn't until years later that this raised any eyebrows. Our passports showed us leaving Australia on a certain day but not arriving anywhere. My passport ended up with a few stamps from a few other countries but it was the Australian tax office of all institutions that queried my status and then not for about five or six years after we left Australia. One particularly officious taxman in Australia seemed to worry about why I had not paid tax for so long and had no proof of address for years. My explanation seemed to make him even more wary.

In that airport lounge we officially made the acquaintance of Valery and Lena Appolovna, my 'secretary' or more correctly my interpreter. This arrangement with Lena began as a nearly full-time job, or at least that was how it was presented to me, but quickly became a much more casual affair.

We saw the block of flats that would be our home. It was a new building and not entirely complete. We were on the 11th floor of a 12-storey block. Here we were greeted by my contact person in the Foreign Affairs Department, Oleg Dadaev. He was an extremely affable and likeable young man. He worked in the Press Centre which was to become a regular haunt, and where press conferences; usually dreary affairs, were held. The flat was full, or seemed to be, with other characters who would be variously significant to us; the comrade from the Red Cross who technically supported us and paid the wages, rather than making it too obviously CPSU largesse, the comrade responsible for housing in the district and so on. It was about seven o'clock

AND SO, TO THE SOVIET UNION

in the morning and we sat down to a huge breakfast, replete with speeches, toasts and vodka. All we wanted was a chance to catch our breaths, rest and possibly have a bit of a look around. Eventually they made their farewells, appointments were made to get things arranged, press cards and the like, and Lena bade us farewell.

Jet lag and days of poor sleep meant that Rose and the children took the lie-down option. I walked with Lena to the Metro station. She gave me a five-kopek piece and a warning to keep on the one line if I wanted to go for a ride on the Metro. It was all colour coded and in theory fool-proof. Something like a deep and meaningful love affair with the Moscow underground was born. Everything everybody has read or described about the grandiose underground stations was true. Our station; Novoslobodskaya, was simply splendid.

The first few days were dizzying. A young woman employed by the International Department helped us with meals and shopping for those days but we felt terribly awkward about the arrangement and soon made the decision to fly solo. We had no idea what we were doing but muddled along. The children were enrolled in their new school, Rose met with her fellow students, I got my press-card sorted out and unpacked a box of things left by my predecessor. A typewriter was the key asset. It was about a third the size of the old machine that had sat on our chest of drawers in Hobart. We were shown how to read our electricity meter, where the nearest shops were and Lena began, inch by inch, to lessen daily contact with us.

Our working lives were beginning but we were still able to ease ourselves in a little. We needed to see Moscow, to feel the place that was so very different to anything we had ever experienced.

Each year a small delegation of Party members spent a month in the Soviet Union, on a sort of rest and recreation leave from the rigours of Party life in Australia. They would spend most of the time in Sochi at one of the sanitoria, enjoying the sun, the water and all that a rather well-set up health resort had to offer. A group was in the Soviet Union when we arrived. Our friend and comrade, Noel Miley was part of this group. When they got back from Sochi after 'lying on the rocks' as he put it, Noel, with something of a proprietorial air that came from having been there two weeks longer than we had, made a point of showing us the sights. It was good to be able to share this time with him as the whole business of what was about to unfold in our lives was just a little bit overwhelming.

We met, after getting hopelessly and helplessly lost, outside a massive children's department store. He was picking up gifts for his children. Our tour through Moscow took us – how could it not – to Red Square. It was night-time. It was a still, chilly evening, and the changing of the guard outside Lenin's Mausoleum, the huge red flag that shimmered over the Kremlin, the cobbles of the square itself all worked a particular magic that never left us. I don't know how many times I walked through Red Square on my way here or there, or simply detoured on my way to somewhere, but it was something that I never tired of. It was Moscow. It was the Revolution. It was socialism. It was the future.

The daily grind

You cannot live your life as a tourist. There is today and today and today. Life goes on and so it did for all of us and as life goes on, so too do challenges arise.

For the children it was at first a huge novelty and so too they were a novelty. There were precious few, or more precisely, no other foreign children that we were ever aware of in ordinary Moscow schools. Language posed a problem but they struggled on. After a time, Louise, the eldest, was taken from high school and enrolled in the preparatory course at Moscow University. When we returned to Australia, she was fluent in

Russian. Brendan's road was a tougher one. He managed to get into bits and pieces of low-level trouble; often courtesy of his new friends. We managed to smooth things over with the relevant house committee and ended up on pretty good terms with all concerned. Teenage boys in the Soviet Union were given a lot of leeway. When they reached the age of 18, they were trundled off into the military for two years and so were allowed a bit of freedom and a deal of leniency beforehand. There was a saying or slogan. We have a privileged 'class' in Soviet society: children. It was pretty much the case. The school system was most successful. Corporal punishment had disappeared many decades earlier. We once saw a harried mother giving a toddler a tap on the bottom on a Metro escalator. She was rounded on by all and sundry with shouts of how dare you strike that child! Outside of school time there were a range of activities run by the Young Pioneers organisation. There were holiday camps. Childcare facilities were free. There was a strong sense of organised freedom, which might sound contradictory, but given the anarchy of 21st century Australia and the alienation of our youth, the Soviet attitude was a breath of fresh air.

Rose's time at the Party school was never going to be easy. She worked hard and then had to come home to the flat, and the children. It was wearing and made more so because of some unnecessary clashes between the students. The 'leader' was unprepared to cut Rose any slack. He had already been the cause of a rift with other students and things got progressively more strained all round. Some of the group would come and visit us to unload. Eventually I was 'shanghaied' into convening a meeting at the school to try and sort out that which was entirely unsortable. There were two distinct factions but the root cause of the problem was that they were all away from everything they knew, understood, or felt that they had any control over. It all came unstuck in any case because about half way through their course they were effectively packed up and sent home. There was a lot of conjecture about this. Some saw it as a break of discipline on the part of the 'leader' who insisted on visiting students from 'illegal' parties who were for security reasons deep undercover and underground. Others saw the hand of Pat Clancy behind it all. There were elements of truth to both stories and Clancy undoubtedly used this indiscretion as a wedge. Clancy's influence was very strong and he was, from all accounts, well pleased with the embarrassment caused.

For Rose this meant a very short break before beginning as a style-editor with the English language newspaper *Moscow News*. There were never enough style-editors in Moscow. Everything, books, magazines, papers, travel guides, shipping journals, was written in Russian and translated by Russians into various languages. The translated work then needed to be tidied up to read and flow well. Rose and one other English speaker did the lot for this weekly paper and a supplement that came with it. Then the other style-editor became ill and was off work for a longish time and could not be replaced. Eventually Rose found a way of exiting *Moscow News* and moved into *Radio Moscow World Service* where she worked for about 18 months before we left the Soviet Union. She loved this work as she had been an actress and had worked extensively in radio in Hobart.

The daily load for me was possibly more routine, or at least ordered. Each day a large envelope, sometimes two, would arrive in my letterbox. This was, of course, in a time when the world was still young and there was no email or internet. The package was the daily collection of TASS reports from the Soviet Union and internationally. I would sift through the 60 or 70 pages for items that could become the basis of my articles for the paper in Sydney. I had to produce all international news as well as occasional magazine-style pieces on Soviet life. As the weeks turned into months this task became less onerous and a lot less time consuming.

Most days would include a telephone call from Oleg in the Press Centre with news of press conferences. For the most part these were tedious affairs. Anything interesting was invariably run with simultaneous translation which pleased my 'secretary' Lena. I was beginning to see less and less of her. Often the most useful part of the press conference round was meeting other correspondents like myself and sharing a café-style lunch with beer that was not Soviet. The local beer sold for 40 kopeks and was unspeakably bad, and even at 40 kopeks was monstrously over-priced. Trolleys of it were wheeled around factories, a bit like the now defunct tea trolleys of an earlier age. The only advantage was that you got a 20-kopek refund on the empties.

I believe that I am the only surviving communist correspondent who worked in the Soviet Union. There might be a German comrade who was only a few years older but apart from him, I can think of nobody who would still be walking this earth. My fellow communist correspondents were almost always much older than me. Moscow was almost a retirement village for ageing communist journalists. My lack of years and of any visible greying of hair or beard did raise a few eyebrows. This was less the case among the other journalists but seemed to puzzle my Soviet hosts, In the early days they frequently remarked on my 'youth' and not entirely in a complimentary fashion. Still, we all got used to each other.

And so, my normal routine played out. Read material, go to press conferences, write the requisite number of articles and send them back to Sydney. The system of despatch was by telegram which, by any stretch of the imagination, was a costly affair. As our expenses were met by the Soviet state, there was a bit of near animosity at the weekly cost of telegramming. How anybody thought I was going to send a couple of thousand words plus the odd 1,200-word magazine article by telegram and not run up a decent bill was beyond my feeble understanding but I was regularly cautioned and advised to do less. All I could do was to ignore the advice. I was doing what I was required by the Party. Good sense finally prevailed and a large and chunky Czech-made telex machine was installed in the flat which made life a lot easier, and certainly a good deal cheaper, but I did miss the physical process of sending the telegrams.

Sending that material had always been a pleasant break for me. We lived about a 25-minute walk to the Central Post Office on Gorky Street. This was about a block from Red Square. I would usually walk via Gorky Street and have coffee when I had finished my telegramming. Sometimes I would take the Metro. This was no less pleasant.

AND SO, TO THE SOVIET UNION

The 'unofficial' embassy and the official Australian embassy

One task that we were expected to perform on a semi-regular basis was to entertain visiting comrades, various travellers, Party and non-Party alike, students and anybody passing through who had been given our address and telephone number. We lost track of the visitors but I think they went away happy enough with their time in Moscow. Apart from anything else, it gave them a chance to spend time in a real Moscow flat.

Flat 46, House 9, Krasnoproletarskaya Street (Street of the red worker or more precisely red proletarian in Russian) was unusual in one respect. We were the only non-Soviet residents among the hundreds who lived there. Most communist correspondents lived as Soviet citizens, but we were spread far and wide across the city. Representatives of the bourgeois media either lived in their respective embassies or in semi-closed groups of flats or compounds

We were in Moscow at the height of the Cold War. The only other Australians to live in the city, or at least as far as we could work out, worked in the Australian Embassy. The ambassador and his wife hosted delegations, as we did. The only difference was that we did not have a staff of Finnish waiters to pass around trays and we did not have drivers to ferry our guests around, but I very much doubt that any of our guests would have wished it otherwise.

When we arrived in Moscow, we didn't register our presence with the embassy. It seemed unnecessary. Our allegiance was not to the Australian state and so our paths did not cross for some time. My first encounter with the embassy was just about the time of the Australian election which ended up returning Bob Hawke. I don't know if the staff there knew we were in town. In all probability they did but nobody mentioned it when I turned up on the step asking about how we might vote. I can't even be sure that we did vote or even that any formal registration of our presence in Moscow was made. We maintained a strange sort of relationship after that.

Possibly because there was nobody else to invite, apart from the usual foreign embassy suspects, Rose and I would get invitations to 'special' events at the embassy. There was an absurdist quality to these soirees. A driver in an embassy car would turn up at our flat and hand deliver an invitation. The driver was a Soviet citizen who would hand the letter over with a rather wry smile. Behind the high degree of official protocol was usually an invitation to celebrate Australia Day which at least had some logic to it but also to Melbourne Cup Day.

AND SO, TO THE SOVIET UNION

Waiters would hand around plates of Four-and-Twenty party pies and cans of Fosters' Lager and all with a studied coolness.

One of these events had two rather different guests. The first was an officially invited guest. John Elliott of Elders IXL fame was in Moscow on some business or other. It coincided with our General-Secretary, Peter Symon, being in Moscow. When I told him that Rose and I had been invited to the embassy, he made it plain that he would like to go as well. I had no idea how this would work out but when we turned up, the three of us were welcomed. Peter was obviously quite taken by this. After Elliott had finished his short speech, Peter told me to go and arrange an interview with him. I didn't know whether to admire Peter's faith in my ability or to question his grip on reality, but I dutifully sidled up to the captain of industry. He was quietly chatting about how he had an interest in wine and had a cellar of a thousand or so reds. He called it a hobby. The 'great man' asked who I was and what I wanted. When I explained, he said to come to his hotel at 11:00 the next morning. He'd give me ten minutes. When I got there, I was told that he's checked out an hour earlier. It's poor form to speak ill of the dead, but really Mr Elliott!

The people we entertained in our not quite so extravagant 'left-embassy' might not have been given any party pies, but a lot of people were fed and watered and I am sure that they felt themselves well pleased. Sometimes we had notice and time to get ourselves organised. Sometimes it was a bit more impromptu. Some occasions stand out and none more so than the time that Spiro Anthony visited. Spiro was at the time the leader of the Young Socialist League in Australia. He was in Moscow to take part in a preparatory meeting for the World Festival of Youth and Students. The normal run of things would be for me to collect the guest or guests, bring them home, have a talk, feed them, and get them safely back to where they were staying. Planning menus was always a bit trickier, especially if we didn't have much warning. It always worked out but this time, the timing was a bit different. Rose was at Radio Moscow. I had a bit on in the morning. Good luck intervened. Rose and her co-workers would often pick up a sort of Soviet version of takeaway. This operated across most workplaces. Lunch was generally the main meal, eaten at a canteen in the workplace. You could then pick up pre-prepared meals and take them home. The word went out on this particular day. 'We have a treat.' Caviar was available. The workers simply lined up with a container; in this case it was a sort of cross between an ice-cream container and a large margarine tub. It was foolishly inexpensive. She was told that it would not keep terribly well.

AND SO, TO THE SOVIET UNION

Dinner for Spiro was caviar and pancakes, followed by more pancakes, jam and ice-cream, all washed down with champagne and cognac. There is nothing, after all, too good for the workers. We never did find out how long a rather large amount of Beluga caviar will last. We never again had such an opportunity.

This element of our life took up really very little time. What it did do was give us a close up look at the Australian abroad. There was the comrade who wanted to find something akin to a late-night club. He was pretty much the worse for wear when he came up with the idea and wouldn't be talked out of it. I got him there, convinced the doorman that he was a visiting communist who didn't really need any special ticket or pass to get in and left him in the doorway. There was the comrade at a book fair who made a fuss about wanting a vodka and orange. The barman was puzzled. Vodka was always served straight. I let the barman pour a bottle of Fanta into a glass and add vodka to it. There was the aboriginal poet that the Party assisted in a tour of the Soviet Union. He fell off the wagon with a spectacular thud. I had to go to the writer's club at midnight to collect him and apologise for him.

Most of our visitors were not like that. There was the charming old comrade who found herself in a pickle about getting a flight home. She was simply passing through as an unassisted tourist. She insisted on taking me to the GUM department store to buy me a ridiculously large and heavy watch as a token of thanks. The watch ran for about as long as it took her to fly back to Australia.

There were, across the three years, a great many people, communists and non-communists who spent time with us. Economist and Sydney academic Ted Wheelwright once spent an evening with us and later we walked him back to his hotel in the heart of Moscow. He was clearly happy to simply hang about with us rather than return to the more formal part of his trip.

Then there was the prolonged stay of George Shenman, from Hobart. He was in Moscow for about three months He would turn up on our door almost weekly. The relationship became, if not strained, a little stretched.

But strained or stretched, George and all the other men and women, communists and non-communists who came our way were welcome. I think that they took away positive memories of the Soviet Union. There was much to feel positive about.

AND SO, TO THE SOVIET UNION

The split in the Party causes a few ripples in our Moscow pond

Things were not always so smooth. The split in the SPA had its effect. That was to be expected. We had been briefed about it and so, when Valery Koudinov, from the International Department told us that 'we are obliged to support you and we will; to the letter, but not beyond' we were not entirely surprised. Lena, my 'secretary', quite out of the blue, chose to tell me how much 'we and I personally admire Pat Clancy very much.' I was a little taken aback but there was nothing to be said that would not further cool an already chilly atmosphere.

We did have a couple of encounters with both Clancy and with Bill Brown. Rose was once invited to share a meal with Clancy at what was called the 'old Party hotel.' A new and ridiculously opulent hotel had been built and Clancy, by dint of his departure from the SPA, did not have access. The meal and the discussion were both just a little uncomfortable, strained and politically loaded.

I received a call to meet with Brown at his hotel. It was an odd sort of meeting. It was in the morning and he was still a little 'blurry' from an obviously long night. We spent about half an hour together on that occasion. We danced around each other for a few minutes before he pointed out to me the errors of my ways and that with the support of the CPSU and trade union support still strongly on 'their' side, I might like to consider my future, or words to that effect. The meeting ended almost cordially. My final comment was something like, we shall have to see what history decides. His reply was a reproach. 'How naïve. I had hoped for something a little more than such a cliché.' It did sting but not for long. Brown and Clancy went on to form the Association for Communist Unity. Brown published a book; they produced a journal for a time and within a few very short years disappeared without a political trace.

Physical encounters with our 'foes' were limited. Our Soviet comrades prided themselves on maintaining protocol, even if that protocol was sometimes a little skewed. We were careful, always to maintain those protocols. I received an invitation to an event at the USSR-Australia Society. The guest speaker was to be Pat Clancy. I left my run a bit late to get there on time. So, I tried to hail a cab outside my local Metro Station. Bad luck often chases bad luck and I couldn't get a cab. It would look bad if I didn't get there, so I approached a militiaman. The Peoples' Militia were the equivalent of our police. I asked his advice and showed him my ticket to the meeting. I stressed that it was important that I get there. He looked at the ticket with the same eye that we saw on so many officials eyes checking tickets or passes – to parades, special functions, state funerals, airports. My 'foreignness' was obvious. I said that I had to be there in 15 minutes. He asked if I was this Pat Clancy whose name was on the ticket. My poor Russian made my answer just vague enough for him to think that I was the speaker. He flagged down a passing taxi and told him to get me there in quick time. To be honest, the driver seemed to enjoy the whole deal.

The event itself was pretty much an anti-climax. Clancy spoke and left. I did manage to meet a young economist whose area of interest was Australia and who, it turned out was well acquainted with the SPA. He had helped edit an economics document for the Party and was in regular contact with Peter Symon. He gave me a copy of his latest book which was about the development of the capitalist economy in Australia. We met frequently. So out of a negative came a positive.

The young economist, Boris Rubstov, introduced Rose and me to his father and mother. Boris Rubstov senior had been a lecturer in Marxist theory and was incensed at the behaviour of the International Department. Whenever I visited his flat, he would turn up the volume of his radio and take me into a corner to talk. It was probably a throw-back to earlier days when 'careless' talk could be a costly mistake, but it was also a sort of metaphor for how things were being played out between the International Department and us.

Being at odds with the line of the CPSU on some issues showed itself in the oddest of places. While in Sochi for our holidays we had some mild words with an interpreter who was working with a small group of comrades from the Irish Party. A couple from the Canadian Party were also present. The 'debate' was over whether we should be too obviously SPA when engaging with the peace movement in Australia. In its own little way, some of the arguments that had caused the split were repeating themselves. Opportunism and 'hiding your light under a bushel', or seeking to win the political leadership of social movements. I put my case but a bit later, out of earshot of the interpreter and guide. These comrades agreed that we should not put our heads, unnecessarily, over the parapet. The message was clear. Don't rock the Soviet boat. It was all so unnecessary. We were staunchly pro-Soviet but believed that we had a right to express a position that best reflected the needs of our Party in our country. This was not a position that was common among other parties.

AND SO, TO THE SOVIET UNION

Beyond Moscow

Had I remained exclusively in Moscow for the full three years, my life would have been busy enough, but the job also involved a degree of travel. This was both domestic and international. The first of these trips, which were called for some obscure reason, 'business trips' was to Kiev and Odessa. The destruction, the butchery on both sides in the Ukraine war, always brings with it an extra level of sadness. There was no sign that things would degenerate into such a morass. People lived and worked as Soviet citizens. It was an attitude that I felt everywhere I went across the whole of the USSR. This has been replaced with so much enmity and despair.

The trip to Kiev was the beginning of a very sharp learning curve. I was invited to the local television studio. I went happily enough. Nobody told me that the reason for my being there, was to be interviewed for a Ukrainian current-events show. There was no preparation time, or idea about what was in store apart from a vague reference to the struggle for global peace. I had been set up. My 'secretary' sat out of shot and smiled. Fortunately, it didn't end too badly. The visit to the Ukraine stayed with me. Odessa and the steps to the sea made so famous by Eisenstein's film, *Battleship Potemkin*, linger in my memory. Whenever I heard of shelling and drone attacks on

Odessa during the Ukraine war, I would wonder about those steps.

Other trips around the Soviet Union took me to various places inside Russia, Kirghizia, Tajikistan, Latvia, and Georgia. I spent time in Volgograd; the scene of the battle of Stalingrad, and a few memorable days in the Jewish Autonomous Region of Birobijan.

Birobijan was in the far east of the Soviet Union and has been variously described as an exercise in national autonomy, or an anti-Semitic policy. The region and its main city had been established in the 1930s to be a homeland for Soviet Jews. It also attracted small numbers of Jews from around the world. When the holocaust was unleashed, the population remained safe. This was an enormous upside although critics maintained that it was originally an attempt by the Soviet Union, still affected by centuries of Russian anti-Semitism, to get the Jewish population out of the way. For my part, I found the area fascinating and the people warm, open and proud of their city and of the life they were living. A simple statistic does give the lie to the 'forced' removal of Soviet Jews theory. By the 1940s there were 50,000 people living in the new city of Birobijan. It is estimated that the Nazis and their collaborators killed two million Soviet Jews. Had there been a forced migration, that the anti-Soviet propagandists maintained, then millions of lives would have been saved.

My other journeys across the Soviet Union were in the company of both communist and bourgeois journalists. There were sometimes moments that showed the Cold War was real. Returning to my hotel in the Kirghiz capital Frunze, now named Bishkek, one night, I saw a group of armed People's Militia, with a dog. They had an American journalist bailed up. One of the militiamen approached me and said, 'comrade, I think the bar is still open or possibly you might like to go to your room.' We left Frunze the following day but the American crew were one short. The journalist had been up to something that annoyed the local officials and was quickly and relatively quietly, deported.

The American news crews and individual journalists in the Soviet Union were there for a political purpose and attitudes were not always warm. The most positive remark I heard from one of the bourgeois American journalists was on an Aeroflot flight about to land in Moscow. The day had been long and trying. It was late at night. Earlier that day we had been on a bus with no air-conditioning in the mountains of Tajikistan. It had been 40 degrees. We flew into Moscow in a blizzard and minus 20 degrees. Visibility was almost nil. Some passengers were getting a little fidgety. One of the Americans loudly declared that on a night like this and with conditions like this the only pilot he would trust was an Aeroflot pilot on an Aeroflot plane. The landing was perfect and a round of applause broke out from his relieved film crew.

Independent travel was not an easy option for us. Our hosts had told us that we would receive all the care due to us but with no 'add-ons.' Rose and I wanted to visit Leningrad. This, of itself, was not an obstacle. Soviet citizens paid hotel fees in roubles and surprisingly few roubles. Foreigners had to pay in foreign currency at much higher rates, or the equivalent in roubles. We had no foreign currency. Our combined monthly salary was 400 roubles; a little over the average of 180 per person. A night's accommodation in Leningrad for a Soviet citizen was certainly no more than 20 roubles. A foreigner had to pay 90 roubles. We went anyway.

Beyond the Soviet Union

Our days were primarily spent in Moscow and our life was set by the routines of work and life. The working visits across the huge Soviet Union added up to a probable total of 30 days or so in total. They were reproduced as magazine articles for the

AND SO, TO THE SOVIET UNION

paper and, on occasion, in other parties' papers and for Novosti news agency.

There were also occasions when I travelled beyond the Soviet Union. The first of these was to the DPRK. It was an odd experience and followed an odd invitation but much that is the DPRK has been described as odd. The phone rang one morning. The caller identified himself as being from the embassy of the DPRK and would it be suitable for someone to visit me. When I said yes, the caller quickly set a time of 10:00am on the following day. I found something to offer my guest and at exactly 10:00am the doorbell rang. My guest turned out to be three guests. They declined any hospitality and so, we sat down and they got immediately to the point. Small talk was clearly not their strong suit. They informed me that there was to be an international meeting of journalists in Pyongyang, asked what 'my impressions were', and would I be coming. To be honest, I wasn't entirely excited at the prospect. I deftly (I thought) got out of making a decision by saying that I would have to discuss this with the Party leadership. They approved of this. The DPRK was still being led by Kim Il Sung – the 'great leader' – and it was logical that I could not act unilaterally. As we parted, they asked when would I be contacting Sydney. I said that evening. They conferred and then said that they would return for my response in two days-time, at 10:00am. I rang Peter Symon that night, hoping that he would say don't bother and that I had work to do in Moscow. He didn't. He told me to go ahead with the trip and that nothing but good could come of it or something like that. It wasn't quite 'what could possibly go wrong', but it could have been.

At 10:00am they rang the bell. They were sure of the outcome and had a preliminary itinerary for me as well as times for my visit to the embassy to get my visa.

The visit lasted about 10 days. The first two of these were spent in bed and being visited about ever three hours by medical staff who injected me with massive doses of vitamins. I had managed to pick up something fairly devastating on the plane from Moscow. My recovery was remarkable. My Korean interpreter informed me that my speech, which I had to hand over for 'translation purposes' was a little short and that I could add to it if I chose. It seemed an odd request and I told him that I was happy with what I had written.

Speakers addressed the meeting in order of their country's place in the alphabet. Australia was not on top of the list but nearly. The first two rows in the auditorium were full of Koreans. At every mention of the 'Great Leader', or his son the 'Dear Leader', they broke into rapturous applause. My speech didn't

AND SO, TO THE SOVIET UNION

mention either by name. I was perplexed as I delivered the speech. About eight times it was interrupted by cheers from the front rows. In the break I discovered that the translated version, in about seven or eight languages included paeans of praise to the 'Great Leader' and to the 'Dear Leader.' It wasn't just me but all speakers were, apparently, spending big chunks of their speaking time doing the same. An American delegate confused things by deliberately leaving his speech behind and ad-libbing.

Despite this the Conference completed its work and we got to see a slice of life in the DPRK. I was offered a trip to the DMZ on the border with South Korea, but in the end no delegate got to make the journey.

The other and undoubtedly more significant trip outside the Soviet Union was to Afghanistan. The possibilities that socialism offered that benighted country were palpable. The war against the US-backed mujahadin was in full swing, although things were said to be relatively stable. An American comrade, Mike Davidow, had been there just a few months before me and had been issued with a Kalashnikov rifle to keep in his room – just in case. My guide while I was in Kabul pointed out a hill on the other side of the city and said that when, rather than if the power goes out at night, it would be because the terrorists would have rocketed the power station. It was a very regular occurrence but he assured me the lights would be back on by dawn. There were a few things that went bump in the night but the power was always on by morning.

It was difficult to telephone Moscow. Rose became concerned when she heard that a plane flying into Kabul from Moscow had been attacked by rocket fire. It coincided with my flight. If a rocket was fired, it missed, but it did make the Moscow news.

I was taken by jeep and with an armed escort to a village about a 45-minute drive from Kabul to visit a group of young and not-so-very young men organised into a self-defence team. These groups had been set up all over the secure parts of the country. That experience was made all the richer for having to stop our little convoy while two old men blocked the road to pray. The time clock for prayers waited for no man. On our way out of the village we heard music. It was a wedding procession wending its way through the ramshackle streets. Decades later I read of another wedding party in Afghanistan. It had been hit by a US missile strike.

I met with a legendary Afghan woman Party leader who had devised a means of educating women in the country. Centres were set up in all villages, The men were suspicious but were invited along to see that their wives were simply being

AND SO, TO THE SOVIET UNION

taught skills that could become a means to bring in some more money. There was always a side room and the door was always open. Eventually the question would be asked about what was inside this room. It was explained that literacy classes were held there. Slowly but almost without fail the men introduced their wives to this room. It was slow. It was a painstaking task, but was having remarkable effects.

Women in Afghanistan at this time were in a period of transition. This was vividly brought home to me when I saw a mother and daughter in Kabul. The younger woman was in Western dress and riding a motorcycle. Her mother, or a woman that I presumed was her mother, was riding pillion but wearing a burqa. So much hope. So much optimism.

The optimism of the people was also tempered with a sense of what might happen if things went wrong. The money, the arms, the training supplied by the USA to the mujahadeen was formidable to say the least. One particular mujahadeen leader, trained and equipped by the USA went on to make quite a name for himself. He was Osama bin Laden. The Soviet army struggled against this guerrilla force and the rest, as they say, is history. My guide and interpreter, like his comrades, was clean shaven. I asked two of them one day how they thought the future would pan out. One paused for a moment and simply said that 'we have to win. We have no time to grow a beard.' It was about as dark a joke as I have heard. I often wonder, about him and his comrades. No beards.

I was in the country to see, learn, report, and also to act as a go-between. The SPA and the Afghan Party, the PDPA, were close. A document was being drafted that would cement this relationship. I was set to meet with the Afghan President Babrak Kamal but he was unavailable. My hosts were apologetic and offered me, instead, an hour with the Prime Minister. I was a bit nervous about the length of time being offered. We met and while I took a few notes, it was hardly an interview. It was a discussion and an enlivening one. To the best of my knowledge, the now former PM, Sultan Ali Keshtmand, is alive and in the UK after gaining political asylum after the fall of his country.

When I got back to Moscow, my American friend, Mike Davidow spoke of Afghanistan and how it must have been like the days after the 1917 Revolution. Separately, we came to weep for the loss; for the loss of both Revolutions.

Most journeys beyond the Soviet Union while possibly significant were less laden with symbolism. I was invited to join the International Organisation of Journalists (IOJ). It was based in Prague and with the invitation came an offer to meet in Prague. It meant a train trip from Moscow to Prague and return. A delightful few days were spent in that splendid city. With my IOJ card in my wallet, I boarded the train, with a German, a Hungarian a Korean and a Pole as companions.

The Polish comrade acted as a sort of tour guide. We travelled through areas on and around the Polish-Soviet border. He told us how, as a young boy in WWII, he had watched the trains carrying soldiers from Germany into the Soviet Union and how a couple of years later he watched many more trains heading home full of wounded and broken German soldiers and how the mood of the people lifted with every train. His family and others in his town had early intelligence of how the Soviet army was destroying fascism.

Moscow as a Muscovite

The memory of the war, the Great Patriotic War, was alive in the Soviet Union. Old men and old women would be asked to tell and re-tell their stories. They, and millions like them stopped the Nazis and won the war. Western historians sometimes like to tell other stories but those veterans whose chests clinked with rows of medals as they walked in parades knew differently.

These men and women were respected by all. They had sacrificed as all Soviet citizens had sacrificed. The sacrifice of the people did not begin and end with the war. The Revolution, the counter-Revolution, the intervention by imperialism that was designed to 'strangle the Bolshevik baby in its cradle' as Churchill so infamously said, the famines, the war, the Cold War, economic isolation by the capitalist world, Reagan's Star Wars, all both steeled the people and simultaneously drained the country and its economy. For more than 70 courageous years the Soviet Union stood tall.

Moscow remains in my memory and remains as both monumental and on a more personal level, as a home, even if only for a short time.

The big-picture memories are of receiving invitations to the Palace of Congresses for major gatherings, where thousands would come together to mark special occasions. These would be preceded by long shuffling queues and repeated scrutiny of passes and checking of credentials before finally gaining admittance. There are images of May Day celebrations and taking my place in Red Square to see the parade that went on for hours. There are images of November 7th parades, again on Red Square and the marching columns of Soviet soldiers, the smell of diesel as trucks, tanks and armour rolled past. The resounding cheers of the troops as they took the salute from the podium atop Lenin's Mausoleum can still be heard in memory.

AND SO, TO THE SOVIET UNION

These events began at dawn. We could hear the bands warming up and when we walked out into the streets near our flat, we would see little knots of marchers and musicians. The atmosphere was always electric and intoxicating.

Then there more sombre occasions, but none the less 'monumental.' Very soon after we arrived in Moscow, the Soviet leader, Leonid Brezhnev died. Rose and I were both in the Palace of Congresses just days before his death. Rose was with the Party school and I was in the press area. We could see him on the other side of the hall and saw him almost slip from sight. He was being propped up by his entourage but the end was very near. Just a few days after our first November 7 celebration, I was again on Red Square at his funeral.

Funerals of leaders became a too frequent pattern. Not that long later I was filing past Yuri Andropov's casket in the Hall of Columns before the funeral on Red Square and again the following year when Konstantin Chernenko died. When Mikhail Gorbachev came to power a macabre thought crossed my mind; either buy a black suit or go back to Australia.

Before Gorbachev's appointment was made, there was a lot of speculation. It was almost as if a sweepstake was taking place about who was the favourite for the job. A Muscovite acquaintance joked that he hoped that an old man would be picked. His reasoning was that an old man had less time to make too many changes and therefore make too many mistakes. He didn't get his wish. Gorbachev was the young leader whose changes saw the end of the Soviet Union.

Life for us, on a day-to-day basis, did not change much, until the coming of Gorbachev. He wanted to break the grip that alcohol abuse had. This was laudable. He set about the task in a foolish way. He ordered the grubbing out of vineyards across the Soviet Union. It was aimed at stopping the production of the cheap and devastating 'port-wine' industry. Vodka and cheap sweet wine were admittedly, a problem, but home-brewing grew as a result. To stop this, sugar was rationed. I was not a home-brewer but remember being loudly denounced by a shop assistant because I had a 500-gram packet of sugar. It was all we needed to buy that day. I slunk away, holding my bag of sugar, feeling almost guilty.

Shopping was always an adventure. Nobody ever left home without a shopping bag. You never knew what special thing you would find. There were always plentiful supplies of all that was needed but often a particular shop would not have something and you had to check in at other places. Heads would bob around doorways and a question would be asked. Do you have eggs or cheese, or whatever. The reply would come, yes or no, depending on circumstances. It was sometimes inconvenient but nobody ever went without. Every day I see the flotsam and jetsam of destroyed, broken lives on the streets in rich Australia. The statistics of homelessness, poverty, food insecurity get worse and yet we are told that socialism didn't work.

Life in Moscow was never easy but always possible. People worked, played, ate out, went to the theatre and movies, and did so with more than a little gusto. We lived as much as a Muscovite family as was possible. We went to the Bolshoi to the ballet, to theatres, to restaurants and little by little, imperceptibly, began to feel at home. It was only when we returned to Australia that we began to feel the alienation, the despair, the lack of potential that goes with life in the West. We didn't recognise it at the time but we were, in ways that really count, freer in Moscow than at any time since.

So many tiny, almost irrelevant things made life rich. The sight of a group of conscripted soldiers making their way through the streets and with the first few rows carefully keeping in step and then seeing the last few stragglers, hand-in-hand as young people did in Moscow, delighted us. To see an elderly woman laden with shopping being reprimanded by a militiaman for not crossing at the lights and seeing two groups of pedestrians taking sides and arguing for and against her until she sighed, picked up her bags and crossed, still against the lights made the sense of ownership that people felt more real than any speech or poster could. To watch, in a restaurant, a family celebrating an anniversary and to see the manic dancing of a balding, sweating man was rewarding. When they discovered that we were foreigners they insisted that we accept a bottle of wine. To be invited into the home of a friend of the children who was soon to begin his military service and to be treated so warmly and so generously was a moment that cannot be repeated.

Our three years sped by. The last year saw Rose still working at *Radio Moscow*. I began writing and presenting a weekly 10-minute segment for radio on my observations on life, politics and international affairs. I was invited to write a book on my time in the USSR. They were busy, sometimes difficult, often troubled times, but so very rewarding and life affirming.

The time came. We took our final trip through Moscow to Sheremetyevo airport. There were many thoughts, clear and confused as we left the Soviet Union. One thing we didn't consider was that in a very few years there would be a capitulation to capitalism. That seemed too fantastic to consider. We gave no thought to the socialist credentials of the Soviet Union. Since the end of the Soviet Union, it has become almost fashionable to do just that.

AND SO, TO THE SOVIET UNION

Retrospective – socialist?

Was the Soviet Union socialist? It was a question that has occupied sections of the left for decades, before and after the collapse. For some it was a socialist state. For others it was 'state capitalist.' Some saw it as neither one thing or another but a society in transition. It might go either way. It certainly ended up going 'one way' although, in retrospect and based both on theory and empirical evidence, I come down unequivocally on the side that says it was socialist.

Some former supporters of the former Soviet Union with a deft move here, a re-phrase there, and a total lack of political shame, simply shifted their allegiance from Moscow to Beijing. Peter Symon once scathingly remarked that the old Soviet leadership just left the room without stopping to pick up their hats. He was right in that estimation. Within months of the collapse of the Soviet Union, many former leading Soviet cadres had become budding capitalists and the slickest among these were destined for greatness in the pantheon of the oligarchs.

Symon was right about them but he was also a little quick in a re-assessment of China and the Chinese Communist Party. He had fought so well and so hard against opportunism only to begin to court China. The SPA became the CPA and today it refuses to see any possible fault with China. There has been a move, a steady move by the Party away from principle in favour of what ...? A peculiar and distasteful abandonment of theory.

It should not be necessary to defend the legacy of the Soviet Union. The 1917 Revolution remains the most significant event of that significant century. The Revolution came to a backward country. It seemed to make a mockery of Marxist theory but the Revolution happened and something rather audacious was attempted and achieved.

There were faults, failings, crimes committed in the name of socialism. It built from a low base and built something that people were justifiably proud of. In the lifetime of one person the country went from peasants using scythes to bring in a harvest and using horse drawn ploughs, to sending people into space. Education was cherished. Life expectancy rates soared. Access to good medical facilities were seen as a right. People were housed and housed well and cheaply. They were confident and assured.

Alienation, anxiety and stress levels were remarkably low. The comparison between Soviet and Australian realities in this area alone hit us like a tonne of bricks when we returned to Sydney. We felt alienated and anxious. I didn't know it, or perhaps would not admit it, but we slid into depressive states when we returned to Australia.

AND SO, TO THE SOVIET UNION

People in the Soviet Union had access to all the things that any decent and modern society should be able to offer. The only difference was that anyone could afford the price of admission. Ballet, opera, theatre; the province of the elite in this country were affordable pursuits for all.

People were not commodified. There were restrictions on 'freedoms.' There was no freedom to exploit. There was no freedom to sexualise women and children, no freedom to write salacious newspaper articles, no pornography, no advertising of useless products, no group in a disordered and dysfunctional society like ours advocating prostitution as something almost 'liberating' for women. These restrictions on freedoms were shining lights, beacons, if you will, of real freedom; the freedom to grow, to feel secure, to know that your children would be well educated, earn their place in the world and live well.

People, when measuring the potential for socialism, when arguing that this or that society is socialist might do well to consider the social in socialism as well as the economic.

The economic factors, however, remain absolutely central to understanding any society. There is always an indissoluble connection between the state and the economic formation that 'feeds' the state. The state is always the state of and for the dominant economic formation. As with the capitalist state, so to with the socialist state. Marxism teaches that the socialist state is temporary as its coercive nature becomes increasingly less a necessity. The Soviet Union had built a socialist economy but was still surrounded by antagonistic, malignant forces that would tear it down. As a consequence, the state had to remain.

The economic proofs of Soviet socialism should not be in question. The planned economy, while often cumbersome, provided for all, but one clinching argument is often overlooked. The producers of all wealth are the working class. Were they exploited? Was it permissible for them to be exploited? It is easy enough to prove. Surplus value from labour produces profit which reproduces capital. What was happening in the Soviet Union? There were no private capitalist enterprises. Any profits derived from labour were returned to the state to be used both for the immediate welfare and sustenance of the workers and to build the state that existed to provide for society as a whole. It is true that there was a layer of relatively well-to-do bureaucrats. But is access to a state-owned car, or the ability to have a dacha in the country quite the same as the capitalist class in this country that wallows in privilege and ostentatious wealth while

AND SO, TO THE SOVIET UNION

people have no homes, where there is poverty, food insecurity, rising crime levels and fear? I don't think it needs answering.

Bu these were not the thoughts that occupied my mind as we began that long flight back to Australia.

Chapter Five

Making a new start

Returning to Australia turned our lives on our heads. Three years away and in such a different world had changed us more than we were able to immediately realise. We had been moving at a pace that was not driven by a capitalist clock. Socialism suited us. Capitalism didn't, but beggars cannot be choosers and we had to adapt. This reality came slowly.

There were immediate and dramatic changes for us. We were to live in Sydney. I was to begin work on the *Guardian* and Rose was to start in the *New Era* bookshop. The Party had arranged a house for us in Redfern, although it was not quite ready. This was not an issue because we had to go back to Hobart to arrange for our things to be sent to Sydney, to see family and visit comrades. People remarked that we looked well. I put this down to the fact that we had just spent a few weeks holiday outside Riga in Latvia and the benefits that come with a health resort. This was undoubtedly true but we were 'well' in a broader sense. It was not to last, as the reality of life in a less caring society took its inevitable toll.

There had been some mild 'looting' of our stored possessions. We discovered this when we got back to Hobart. This was a bit disappointing. We saw evidence of bits and pieces of our not altogether substantial belongings in Hobart and later in Sydney. One particular 'comrade' who had moved to Sydney seemed to think that we were not coming back. We were not best pleased and did not make an issue of it.

I left Hobart before Rose. At the time trading ships worked the coast of Australia. The Seamen's Union crewed these ships and it was easy enough to arrange transport. It was a practice known as 'ring-bolting.' The term comes from the metal bolt that was used to secure a ship to its mooring. Legend has it, and it seems to be true, that the gap or cavity where this cable was stored was now and then used to hide illegal passengers. In the latter part of the 20th century, it simply meant that an 'illegal' passenger was brought on board. There were only two conditions that applied. The first was that the 'ringbolt' must be acceptable to the crew or at least to the union delegate. The second related to what could be carried. You could take whatever you could carry up the gangplank. The system worked well and especially for transporting people like me across bodies of water when airfares were still rather expensive. It had been a regular practice for many years. Sadly, one of my comrades managed to spoil the arrangement. I heard that he had attempted to take a car with him.

The practice was unofficial and the captain and officers were not supposed to know what was going on. Blind eyes were turned all round. My trip went well. The ship made very good time and as we were about to pass Wollongong, very early in the morning, a message came from the bridge telling the crew that we would be moving close to the shoreline so 'your ringbolt can enjoy the view.'

Back in Sydney I was introduced to our new home. It was the top floor of an old terrace house in Redfern. The bottom half was leased to a Cypriot couple who ran a restaurant. The arrangement worked well. We met only once or twice. The landlord, Tom Costa, was a Party member. Tom agreed to a very low rent. His children, Con and Dorothy were activists in the Young Socialist League and remain today staunch Marxist-Leninists and leaders of a new party that has broken from the CPA; the New Communist Party of Australia. Tom raised his children well.

MAKING A NEW START

Those first months back in Australia were erratic for us. We liked the work. We enjoyed being back in a branch of the Party, but at the same time we were disoriented. I had difficulties in becoming part of a collective. By this I mean the editorial collective. I did my work happily enough but found the editorial meetings difficult. For years I had worked very much alone. I became withdrawn and emotionally a little isolated. I could not work out what was going on with me but I was aware that I was becoming unhappy. I did not know it but I was simply depressed. The sense of loss that I felt after leaving Moscow was unconscious but real.

Rose was very much in the same boat. She saw a doctor. He had once lived in the GDR. He explained to Rose that she had lost her 'protective' psychological shell. She had not needed it in Moscow. He assured her that it would grow back, and in a most insightful way said that what she needed he could not prescribe. The curative was to go back to socialism. We couldn't.

The lack of care for people, the alienated youth, the despair that was all around us was at the core of this problem. That was a long time ago. The disintegration, the degradation, the collapse of capitalism and with it the collapse of the old verities, even if they were false ones, has made this country a miserable one where half-lives are eked out.

But, in the mid-1980s we had work to do and lived as best as we could.

Despite the 'disorientation' we became active again and engaged in some rather memorable activities. The Party had suffered from the split, but there was still a very strong sense of optimism. Just as we were beginning to get settled a rather ambitious multicultural concert took place. It involved comrades from a broad range of ethnic backgrounds; Turks, Lebanese, Iraqis, Iranians, Greeks, Chileans and Anglo-Australians. Poetry, song, dance, all on the theme of the struggle for peace and socialism. Rose and I became involved. We both had experience in theatre and were pretty much co-opted. It was a remarkable evening. Hundreds of people filled the Tom Mann theatre in Surry Hills to share a common desire to build a movement for change.

A bit further down the track we became involved in launching a campaign in Redfern against the intrusion of the racist National Action. They were both the continuer of earlier fascist organisations in Australia and the forerunner of the National Socialist Movement that emerged more recently. They had been postering around the area. A few YSL members set out with stencils and paint to put a different perspective. The police intervened. They fled but one of their number, our son, wasn't fleet enough of foot and was taken to the Redfern police station. The Redfern police had a certain reputation. A member of the YSL group rushed to our place with the news. We managed to get Brendan home safe but it was clear that the police were itching to provoke something. A wrong word would have seen him charged and held in a cell. By the time of our next branch meeting the idea of a campaign had been hatched.

About a dozen or so of us took to the streets with leaflets and pots of white paint. We called it the 'Redfern White Out' campaign. We simply painted out racist slogans and talked to the locals about what we were doing and why. This led to a petition campaign and a successful public meeting in the Redfern Town Hall. Al Grasby, a former minister in the Whitlam government and one of the architects of the policy of multiculturalism in Australia, was an enthusiastic speaker at the meeting.

We spent the best part of two years in Sydney. They were the best and worst of times for us. We were committed to the movement and to socialism but I 'found' all manner of faults in the Party. In retrospect, these had more to do with me than the Party, and tied to an on-going low-level depression. There were nascent, embryonic factions emerging in the Party. A new 'Broad-Left' grouping was beginning to emerge. This was populated largely by ex-SPA members as well as old CPA forces who could see their own organisation crumbling. Some friends of ours, within our branch, and in other branches, were secretly courting the new group. Another small group were promoting ideas of a decidedly 'leftist' bent. All the battles that had been fought when we first became members appeared to be re-emerging. We were becoming more than a little disillusioned.

Retreat

We probably read more into this than it deserved, but it fuelled a dissatisfaction in me. Rose and I resolved to leave Sydney and return to Hobart. We were becoming more and more estranged from the Party. Wanting to move was one thing. Finding the financial resources to make such a move was quite another. Party functionaries do not become wealthy. Our Party wage was enough for us to get by and we got by, but there was no fat; no savings and no way that any could grow. It was an awkward position. We had to find new jobs and by this time, they were not exactly falling from the trees. The 'official' unemployment rate was close to eight per cent. The reality was far greater. People queued to put in their dole forms each fortnight.

Rose left the bookshop. She worked briefly as a telemarketer before getting a job with a local hospital in Redfern. It was arduous work but she did earn more than she was getting at *New Era*. The great edifice that was the bookshop did not have all much longer in it before it crumbled and collapsed under the weight of intolerable debt. It stood at one time as a beacon of socialist optimism. It was a folly and remains in our memory as a symbol of what was to come.

It took me a little longer to extricate myself from the *Guardian*. I ended up in an accountant's office. It was one of those monstrous globally-controlled and owned operations that specialised in insolvency and business bankruptcies. These were boom times for such an outfit. I was taken on as a records clerk. Why me, I couldn't say. Perhaps they sniffed an air of desperation about me. My tasks were spectacularly mundane but it allowed me the chance to get a whole new insight into Marx's teachings on labour and value. The action of taking something from a file or moving something to another file took mere seconds. These seconds, like all activities in the office were given a 'value' and had to be charged to the client. In my case the seconds had to be charged as well. The entire Kafkaesque operation was obsessed with charging five minutes here, twenty minutes there. I probably spent about twenty per cent of my day adding my charges to lists for another department to move somewhere else.

We finally scraped up the cost of getting us back to Hobart. The next period in our disjointed lives was spent moving from rented house to rented house. This had been our way for as long as we had been together. I got bits and pieces of work. Rose managed to get back into voice-over work for radio and television. We did a bit of acting. I supplemented my dole with a couple of days taxi-driving each week. It was pretty much a hand-to-mouth existence but we didn't seem to notice, or so it seems from the distance of time. This went on, relatively aimlessly for about 18 months until I got something of a lucky break.

The Education Department had begun an Asian Studies project. I got the job of writing and editing a small monthly magazine and occasionally writings scripts and presenting these, on-camera, for a companion ABC TV series. Getting the job and the interview process was an odd affair. Nobody asked, so I didn't say, about what I had been doing for the past several years. Before Moscow I had been a teacher, but even this didn't seem relevant. Either nobody cared or everybody knew. Hobart is, after all, a small place. I will never know and it hardly matters. I was simply asked if I could do the job. I said yes. They said, here is an idea that we want you to write about. Bring it back in the morning. It was a light piece about something to do with Japan as I remember. I took it back the next day. They had a cursory read of it and said, are you right to start on Monday. Their current writer was leaving that Friday.

It all went along well enough for the next 18 months or so. The only problem was that the project had a finite life-span. An opportunity came up for me to do some postgraduate study at Griffith University in Brisbane. It was in the same Asian studies area. Once more we left Hobart.

We spent a year in Brisbane and this put us back into close contact with the Party.

Brisbane

My course at Griffith was to lead to a Masters' Degree in Asian and International Studies. It made sense, given the trajectory that my life had taken. Things went surprisingly well. The head of the unit had begun discussing with me about what I would like to focus on for my thesis and there were strong hints at a PhD. Plans were well under way for some part-time teaching to make it all financially viable. At this stage I was on AUSTUDY payments and Rose was drawing the dole. Financially things were incredibly tight. The joint income was less than a married couple's unemployment benefit.

The course was coming to an end. All results were in bar one unit on economics. Then the wheels fell off in grand old style. I got very sick. I needed to score something like 45 per cent in a final examination for this last unit. It was a formality, but I could barely focus when I sat the exam and fell two per cent short. Days passed before I was sent off to have another shot. By then I was even sicker and again the result fell magically short. Despite plans for me to quickly knock over the unit in the following semester, our funds had dried up. We were faced with a decision and Sydney looked to be the answer.

The year spent in study was also a year spent back in a branch of the Party. When we arrived in Brisbane the SPA had a formal office. Ray Fergusson was still the secretary and things gave the appearance of stability. Within months that had all changed. I missed a couple of months due to settling into Brisbane life and to study. Nobody seemed all that keen about talking of the changes that had taken place. The office and centre had ceased to be. The branch, much smaller, was meeting in the living room of the new branch secretary. Fergusson and some other familiar faces were no longer around. Even though I had a long history in the Party, I was clearly not to be taken into anyone's particular confidence, and the Party had and has still a tendency to cut out of collective memory anyone who is no longer a part of the organisation. It is not one of their more endearing features.

The now tiny group battled on as best they could. We attended rallies, sought to sell a few papers, had meetings and enjoyed a rather warm relationship with the Brisbane branch of the SWP. This aspect of things was rather intriguing. The SWP seemed happy enough with the arrangement as did my comrades but it was all so reminiscent of meetings that I had been aware of in Sydney only a few years earlier between the leaderships of both parties. There had been a serious attempt at some semi-official fusion of the two formerly bitter enemies. It was disturbing at the time and seemed to indicate a rather dramatic shift from the principled position of the struggle around the Fourth Congress and the attempt to build a Party free of opportunist tendencies.

It was more than appropriate for the branches of the two parties in Brisbane to work together on areas of common interest but at the back of it all lay the Soviet Union and its looming demise. It seemed that everywhere I went the talk was pretty much the same. Older comrades, in particular were expressing concern at what was looming. These veteran SPA members had devoted their entire lives to the cause of socialism and had done so willingly. There had always been a special light on the hill. The Soviet Union was that special place where the working people just like themselves had taken power and built something memorable.

This sense of the coming implosion seemed to have an expression, if unstated in the Party in Sydney when we returned in early 1992. The Soviet Union ended as we were packing up to leave Brisbane.

Back in Sydney

The Party still went about its work although there was a decided lack of any real spark in the air. The Party Centre in Campbell Street was decidedly shabby. Work needed to be done to repair this and that but it was either ignored or poked at in a perfunctory manner. The YSL had ceased to function. There were none of the trappings of old. No symbolic gatherings, not even a false or misplaced triumphalism. Still, this was 'home' and we did our best to settle in.

Rose and I moved into a little conjoined place in Newtown. We had nothing. Our possessions were few. This was how we had lived our lives and we saw nothing special about it. The years had been moving on but life was still manageable for

MAKING A NEW START

those with little. The icy chill of late capitalism, the collapse of the welfare state, the winding back of services and all the rest of the neoliberal nightmare was happening but not yet to us.

Earning a living soon proved to be a problem. Rose, who had once been employed in the extravagant *New Era* bookshop, set up with Peter Symon's support, a tiny room just inside the front entrance to the Party building as a bookshop. It went by the name of *SPA Books*. She worked there on a commission basis. It didn't make her wealthy but it helped both the Party and also added to our dismal coffers. I would drop in on a fairly regular basis. The walls were thin and Rose's shop shared such a thin wall with the *Guardian* editorial office. I made it a regular practice to be in the shop when the editorial meeting took place. There was an often, unrestrained animosity between members. Differences were always sorted out, but never, it seemed, amicably. The meeting would usually erupt with a high degree of invective and then a simmering discontent hung over the group. Not many years had separated me from these meetings. They bore no relation to what I had remembered. Civility had long since left the building.

I was unable to find work. Things were beginning to look less than bright when a break came my way. It came via the *New Era* warehouse. While the *New Era* shop had closed down, the rather big warehouse still operated. It was now selling art books and coffee-table books from the now former Soviet Union and from other publishers. The warehouse had a full-time storeman/packer/despatcher. He was rather unwell. Much of this was self-inflicted. He drank too much and smoked too much. He had frequent and occasionally long stints in hospital. I was offered the job of holding the fort in his absence and helping out when he was at work. This suited everybody concerned. I was given a daily, cash-in-hand payment that supported the dole. I was also given a 20-minute crash course in how to drive the fork-lift, shown how to prepare the orders and was pretty much left to my own devices.

The debt to Moscow and Mezhdunarodnaya Kniga, or International Books, was formidable. 'Mezhkniga' had not pressed for payment but with the end of the Soviet Union came a new and more dollar-focused operation. The new 'management' in Moscow had already put to bed any old-fashioned notions of proletarian internationalism. The new order was a chilly one. The piper was keen to be paid. This meant an end to *New Era*.

The poor health of the SPA soon became a little clearer, and in a sadly symbolic manner. It was nothing 'political' as such. It was an annual event; the *Guardian* Festival. We had attended our first festival not long after our return from

Moscow. I remember well the rows of stalls, the music, the performers and the quite substantial crowds. It had been a great success. After the day in the park a concert was held in the Enmore Theatre. A visiting group of Soviet entertainers was the draw. I had been railroaded into being the MC for this show. It was a simple business of introducing each act, very much as any similar show would have been conducted back in the Soviet Union. I was given the job for the simple reason that I had a relatively new suit, or at least that was what I was told when the organiser smilingly gave me about three hours-notice of the job.

I had those images in my mind as we headed off to the 1992 *Guardian* Festival. It was in a park that seemed particularly big, but only because the 'festival' occupied so little space. A few meagre stalls did a meagre trade. A couple of singers sang to a tiny audience. It had nothing in common with the Festival of memory.

Bob Gould, the late proprietor of the legendary *Gould's Bookshop* in Newtown was there and he made a cruel, cutting, but darkly apt comment. A Russian woman with a child in a pram had been walking through the park. She had little, if any, interest in what was going on. One of our comrades spoke to her and discovered that she was from the former Soviet Union. A member of the tiny Trotskyist group, the Spartacist League, also spotted her and sought to draw her into an unwilling conversation which led to 'words' being exchanged. Gould smiled, or possibly smirked and said 'look, the dead arguing with the mad.' Sadly, that image stayed with me much longer than it would have for Bob Gould.

Reality was beginning to nip at our heels. Money was about to become a very real issue. *New Era* was in its very last days. The date was set and my time, as probably the worst forklift driver in the southern hemisphere, came to an end. We needed to make a decision. I needed work but wasn't getting any. The walls were beginning to close in. We made the choice to return again to Hobart. We often look back on that decision and regret it, but economics always plays a dominant role. It is, after all a cornerstone of Marxist theory; that economic structures and actions tend to motivate political reactions. However, theory was not in the forefront of our minds. Survival was. And so, we packed up once more.

The wilderness years

What followed was a period, and an extended period, of isolation and introspection. It was a period of 'making do', of settling for something and a life that we never really wanted and which did us no good. It did allow us to keep the wolf from the door and gave us 'security' in an insecure world. It allowed us the chance to move into older age with fewer real economic fears, but at a certain cost.

In my earlier life I had been a teacher. I had no desire to be one again but I sort of fell back into the job. It started by my doing a little relief-teaching while I looked for a job. A casual teacher's job turned up. It led to another and I became, once more an employee of the Tasmanian Education Department.

The old fable tells of the ant and the grasshopper. We all know how it goes. A morality tale to urge us to settle to a task, put away for a rainy day and ultimately 'behave.' Rose and I had long been 'grasshoppers' and we liked it that way. We had seen 'ants' and had never wanted that sort of life. There was a piece of wall graffiti that I passed regularly. Its message of 'consume, be silent and die' seemed to say it all. Things had been going on in the world and the crisis of capitalism was beginning to sharpen. To make matters worse, when I looked at the horizon, I saw my 40th birthday looming.

The significance of this date was simple. We had no resources and few 'visible means of support.' The golden age of capitalism had built the welfare state and a general degree of prosperity, coupled with a pause in the global fall in the rate of profit allowed for something almost like largesse on the part of the state. The 'good times' were never going to last, although the crash caught us all out. The golden age was an aberrant time. Capitalism and its state have never willingly handed over anything to anyone. The same golden age, it needs to be remembered, was built on the bones of 80 million deaths in WWII. That figure represented 3.8 per cent of the entire global population in 1940. A golden age indeed.

What was happening as that significant birthday drew closer was a retreat of capital. In the 1970s and 1980s came neoliberalism. It was characterised by the infamous saying of Margaret Thatcher that there is 'no such thing as society.' A long period ensued whereby people were separated, one from another, where the collective became the individual, where society became atomised. The 1980s in Australia were the years of the Hawke and Keating governments, the Accord, class collaboration, all in the name of saving and serving capitalism.

It was a time which saw skilled workers become 'self-employed.' It was a time where solidarity between the class was shattered into a million individual pieces, all competing with one another for the crumbs that fell their way.

This was also a time when capitalist profitability was once more threatened. It was the period that drove capital to relocate entire industries to low wage regimes to boost profits while destroying entire economies along the way. Globalisation didn't save capital. Today we live with the rebound of economic nationalism, trade wars, tariffs, war, and the constant threat of war.

From the 1980s the crisis meant a dramatic shift in what had become a comfortable approach to things. Work was, at first scarce and then, as the years rolled by, secure work was increasingly replaced by the gig economy and an insecurity that was devastating. No part of life was untouched by this. Rents were rising. Once people like us could simply move at will. A fierce competitiveness in the 'market' was destroying all this. It was becoming clear that we had to knuckle down, get a mortgage and become 'ants.'

What followed was a period of a decade or more working for the Tasmanian Education Department as a high school teacher. My tenure was, for a few years, limited. To achieve anything like 'security' there had to be three continuous years of service. Each 'temporary position' was limited to one year. If staffing levels permitted, then another year, or few months might be added on. A break in service meant that the three-year period would have to begin again. Teachers had imagined for decades that they had little in common with other workers. Reality was beginning to strike home.

Each year I would have to do the rounds, looking for another job. We travelled, almost in a circle around Tasmania. The pay kept coming but so too did the removalists fees as we wandered across the island. Finally, I managed to get the illusive 'permanency' tag. This also meant that we could return to Hobart.

A serious downturn in the economy meant that there was a period in Tasmania where housing prices were depressed. We were now a few years older. The magic 40th birthday had passed but we did, finally stop being renters. It was a two-edged sword. We had never lived a suburban existence. Admittedly the little house was close to the beach and handy to things, but life was an almost self-imposed exile. At first, we welcomed this change, or possibly we just pretended to ourselves that we did. Our political bridges seemed to have been burned, but so too our horizons became lowered. There was nothing we could do about this. Life in capitalist, neoliberal Australia was not for ageing 'grasshoppers.' What would happen to us if we found ourselves pensioners with no resources to keep out the chill of this cruel and uncaring society.

And so, the years went by. We observed political things but from afar. We had no contacts with the left. We figuratively disappeared from view.

My life as a teacher was not a fulfilling one. I was never one of those who were born to do the job; never one of those with a vocation. It was always a struggle. My fellow-teachers were, by-and-large, crushed or bruised by their life and work. There was little stimulation, little discussion of anything beyond the gates of the school. The staff-rooms in the schools I worked in were dour places. I found myself, like so many of the others around me, keeping a regular eye on my superannuation account and also on the calendar. I was entitled to cash in my super not long after I turned 55. Most of my colleagues cashed in their chips on that magical birthday and disappeared into retirement. For the 'lifers' this meant a very comfortable retirement. The entitlements were generous. I had nowhere near enough in my account as I had started later but there was enough to pay off the relatively small mortgage. I 'retired' although I had to immediately begin relief teaching to make ends meet.

I had been desperate to leave teaching behind me but time hung heavily on me. Rose became anxious about me. I was becoming depressed. She then made a suggestion that both elevated my mood and gave my life a new direction. I was to return to study.

A re-awakening

Many years earlier I had attempted postgraduate study in Brisbane. It nearly worked but the fates did not smile upon me. My new foray into the world of academia was to end with a little more success.

I had been unaware that any such opportunity existed, or rather that such an opportunity could be attempted without immediate and crippling financial cost. At Rose's urging I began looking at what was possible. A number of universities were offering courses that could be conducted on-line. Any such course came with a HECS debt but that was another issue entirely. I found a university offering a course in International Relations. It seemed an idea whose time had come and was too good to pass up. The very worst outcome was that I would fail. The course was in segments; a Graduate Diploma, or if results were good enough, entry into an MA course. Further on was the alluring carrot of being able to write a PhD thesis.

There were probably 100 students studying each of the units in the course. Some were working and looking to get promotions in Foreign Affairs or non-governmental organisations, some were students continuing after their undergraduate work, and possibly two or three were like me. For the bulk of the students, it was a case of saying and doing the 'right' thing at all costs to get the right result for the right outcome. It is a sad reflection of the commodification of society that education for itself and for its own sake is long dead. For me there was never going to be any pot of gold at the end of the rainbow; no glittering prize. But it was all rather liberating. I could say what I wanted to say, write what I believed to be appropriate, and most importantly of all, focus on a theory that had long been lacking in my life.

Every unit in the course was able to be approached from this or that aspect of Marxist theory. I began to learn, to test my ideas, and to dispute with others. The PhD thesis gave me full scope to study, write and consider Marxist theory for over two years in an uninterrupted fashion. Decades earlier, Peter Symon, in our flat in Moscow had wistfully commented that he would like to have the entire membership of the Party in full-time study for a year. That could never happen. I was far luckier, although the good fortune didn't come until rather late.

The PhD was a defence of Marxism. It examined the crisis in capitalism and the corresponding crisis in Marxist theory, which aided and abetted what appeared to be capitalist 'resilience.' In defending the idea, I had to engage with a long trend of decay and obfuscation among those who have distorted Marxist theory for more than a century. What began as a response to capitalism's capacity to withstand crisis in the 1930s and a fear of Marxism's centre shifting away from Berlin to Moscow gathered pace as each new school of thinkers dismantled more of Marx. The central role of the working class was gradually eroded. New sources were heralded as the 'revolutionary' force. The broadly oppressed or disadvantaged, the unemployed, the marginalised in society, were all in their turn to be regarded as the force that will challenge and defeat capital.

As decade followed decade and capital survived, the 'theorists' became more desperate, despairing and demoralised. Perhaps the answer might lie in the national liberation movements and anti-colonial struggles. Perhaps it was the student radicalisation of the 1960s, the black liberation movement, or the women's movement. The deterioration in the thinking of these 'academic Marxists' gathered pace. The Frankfurt School and

Western Marxism quietly amalgamated with the newer, more fashionable salons of the New Left which put on fresh garb as Eurocommunism. The clever thinking adapted the philosophy of the day into an absurd caricature of Marxism. Postmodernism was able to be reconfigured as 'post-Marxist Marxism.' The politics of identity came upon the land and all that remained was a residual adherence to the working class as the revolutionary class, and even this was effectively relegated to library shelves or as an historical footnote. Engels had to be decoupled from Marx and was portrayed as the 'reason' Marxism did not live up to its potential.

I read, I thought, I went back to Marx and to Engels and to the classic Marxist writers and learned. It was a political awakening or rather re-awakening. By the time the thesis was completed, I felt confident to stand and call myself a Marxist! This journey was conducted in isolation. There were no comrades that I could share ideas with. The barren years of earning a living as a teacher in various parts of apolitical Tasmania kept me ignorant of what was happening to a left that existed beyond the walls of academe. This was the height of naivete. Theory and practice. Practice and theory. If the theory had gone so far astray, why would not the practice of socialist politics be just as poisoned? I was ignorant of this and somehow clung to the notion that those fighting for socialism and revolutionary change were able to hold the theoretical and ideological line. What I failed to include in my calculations was that the political manifestations of Marxism had never been particularly well-equipped with theory and that they were just as likely to be affected by the fashionable affectations of what it meant to be 'progressive.' I was in for a rude awakening.

Chapter Six

Looking for 'home'

There seemed no real point in our staying any longer in Hobart. We did a few rudimentary calculations, sold our house, drove to the other end of the island and caught the ferry to Melbourne. Our motivations for getting rid of our house, becoming tenants again and moving to Melbourne would have been questioned by some. We were heading into a relative unknown. If the truth be told, we wanted another throw of the dice. We had been stuck for too long in a life-style that was alien to us. Political ideas had been tamped down for far too long and things were beginning to bubble once more.

The political re-awakening had a lot to do with my return to study and to my immersion in Marxist political theory and economics. At the end of the extended study period, I was technically a political economist and international relations theorist. I was just about too old to expect to hang up my 'shingle' and there seemed nowhere for me to hang my political hat. We had resumed reading the various left-wing newspapers and websites. Much of what we read was less than satisfying, but I hoped for better and tried to 'read into' things, that which was probably not there but which I tried to make fit my world view. This was, in reality a mistake and decidedly un-Marxist. Objective reality, guided by a degree of empirical evidence and supported by analysis and all based on theory is always better than any subjective assessment. What we want things to be is not the same as what they actually are.

We settled in Melbourne. Our actions in those first months were spent as almost left-wing tourists. We were reading more, went to occasional rallies and public meetings hosted by different groups. This was in 2019. We attended one massive event. It was the Global Climate Strike. This rally of 100,000 people in Melbourne was at once enlivening and also signalled a warning. The strength in numbers and sentiment was powerful. It was just four months into the term of the Scott Morrison Coalition government. The anger of the people was directed at him, his government and their refusal to act. There was a feeling that all that was needed was to remove an individual and 'hey-presto' all would be fixed. The ALP and Anthony Albanese were shielded from criticism. The banners, the placards, the speeches tended to follow this line. The left was there and their propaganda, their banners, were little better. Still, the memory we took from that day was of the power of the people in their thousands and the anger that they felt.

This was a period that saw massive unrest across all continents. The streets of all cities were wreathed in tear gas as the people fought for a better way. Seemingly small things; a rise in train fares, a problem with mobile phone charges, saw an eruption of class anger aimed at the real targets and the real issues. Bigger issues; rising pensions, and cuts in social welfare, saw hundreds of thousands in cities and towns across the world in action. All that was missing in so many of these struggles was a political leadership. Whether any of these moments could be described as revolutionary moments, or pre-revolutionary moments is by-the-by. The anger was there and it was not able to be appeased. And then a tidal wave hit the world. Covid.

The pandemic closed borders, sealed states, slowed economies and put a halt to interactions, locally, nationally and internationally. This was a necessity. Our early forays out and about and onto the fringes of political life came to an abrupt halt. I kept on writing. A couple of books managed to be published. These were extensions of my original book that flowed from the PhD. I also contributed on a semi-regular basis to the public policy journal *Pearls and Irritations*, and to the journal *Independent Australia*. As lock-downs came and went, so too did opportunities for the left to get out, if briefly. We took advantage of these moments as well. There were rallies in support of Assange. I was invited to speak at a rally against the drive to war with China.

In 2021 Rose and I took the decision to move from Melbourne to Geelong. There was a lull in Covid and health issues made the move logical. The rate of infection was marginally less. It was in Geelong that we became a little more closely involved in left politics.

By a trick of fate, the Socialist Alliance had come to dominate the left in Geelong. The Alliance had come into existence after a long and rather convoluted journey. The old Socialist Workers Party had shifted course and ideological perspective a number of times and had evolved or morphed into the Democratic Socialist Party. This group then sought a regrouping of a range of small and smaller left parties and groups into a new and broad Socialist Alliance. There were a number of takers. Some were surprised at this. Less surprising was the quick disintegration of the new broad left movement. In a very short time, the Socialist Alliance came to be made up of the now-defunct

Democratic Socialist Party and a handful of independent supporters. It continues to exist, fields candidates in elections and goes through its paces as an eco-socialist party. It champions all the fashionable identity-driven causes. The Geelong operation grew rapidly in its early days and still has quite a few members.

We came into close contact with the Alliance. There was a sense of nostalgia in this. It took us back to more innocent times, the old SWP and its earlier manifestations. I wrote for their newspaper, *Green Left* for the better part of a year. It was hardly a match made in heaven. The Alliance was and is very much a 'let all flowers bloom' operation. Articles in the paper would often contradict each other. There was no clear position on anything. I had been looking for somewhere to call 'home' but this was such an eclectic mix of ideas that our paths soon diverged.

I returned to writing for the two journals, *Pearls and Irritations* and *Independent Australia*, while continuing to read the left press, including my old paper, the *Guardian*. It was during this period that I discovered that an article of mine from *Pearls and Irritations* had been re-printed in the *Guardian*. The editors of each publication had agreed to this. I hadn't been involved in the negotiations but had no problems with the decision. It was not all that long after that an at first tentative relationship began between the *Guardian* and me.

A return to the CPA

I was asked if I would give permission for occasional articles to be re-published in the *Guardian*. I was happy enough with this but it did puzzle me just a little that I was being asked after the event. I made an offer, a month or so further on to 'cut out the middleman' and submit occasional pieces for the paper that seemed appropriate. I was a little surprised at how readily this offer was accepted. The paper, after all, is the official organ of the CPA. When I thought back to my former days with the paper, no such arrangements would have been conceivable. The only way a non-member was printed was via a letter to the editor. This puzzled me and in retrospect it ought to have sounded an alarm bell. It didn't.

This casual arrangement continued for a time. My contributions became more regular. I would send something almost every week and most were getting an airing. I began a sort of correspondence with the editor of the paper and found that he worked out of Melbourne. Things and times had changed. I was still operating on an old formula; where an editorial collective worked out of the office in Sydney. I got my head around things but it seemed somehow a poorer world and less satisfactory.

Our ever-so-slightly arms-length relationship went on for some time. Slowly I heard of this and that old comrade who was still in the Party. Many had died or had seemed to have just slipped away. They appeared to have been forgotten. I didn't pay much attention to this. I was delighted to hear of the few who I remembered from my past. No actual contact was made, but the editor of the paper would pass my greetings on.

I was in Geelong and a range of issues made regular travel between Geelong and Melbourne difficult. A branch of the Party was 'active' in Melbourne. I met with comrades from this branch on a couple of occasions. I don't know what I expected. I went to Melbourne for May Day and found the Party stall. There were about four members in evidence. When the march got underway, I found the banner and another three or four members. I wondered at this but I was already in the process of hitching, or possibly re-hitching my wagon to the Party star and so didn't wonder as much I might have or should have. By the time of the anniversary of the Russian Revolution I was ready to commit to the Party and so, again, didn't pay proper attention to the fact that about a dozen people attended that celebration.

Most of my efforts for the Party revolved around writing for the paper. The occasional article turned into a regular piece and this grew. I saw this as a responsibility. My usual contribution became four or five articles a week. I attended meetings via zoom. They were a little listless and quite poorly attended. When I joined, I was obliged to undergo, also via zoom, an 'induction' class. I was more than happy to do so. I naively thought that this would be an initial class as part of an on-going and regular series of classes. I naively believed that the Party was attending to the theoretical training of its members. Two other new recruits and I were talked through the Party Constitution and a few questions were asked of us. It seemed an odd way to begin. What became odder was that there were no more classes. There was, at the end of the following year, a weekend 'school.' By this time, I had been a member for nearly two years. Two days of education in two years seemed to highlight the problems that I was feeling.

My concerns at the direction of the Party were initially centred around my branch. It was never easy to see what was happening in other branches in other States. From a distance, things seemed to be healthier. What I discovered later was that Melbourne was no better or worse than anywhere. Much of the problem lay in the central leadership, but so much more lay, not so much as a drift into opportunism, but an enthusiastic embrace of it. It is almost impossible for this not to happen when the best the Party can offer is a perfunctory two-days of education in two years.

At about the time that I getting ready to exit the Party, a National Cadre School was being organised. A small group of comrades were to spend a few days at a residential 'camp' over the Easter long weekend. This ought to have been encouraging, but it was made clear that 'nominations' for places would be closely vetted by the leadership. The three or four days as the brochure declared were to assist comrades achieve a 'mastery' of Marxism-Leninism. Mastery indeed. This 'finishing school' was coming hot on the heels of an almost total neglect of any theoretical or educational work. To be fair, there might have been the occasional class in an occasional branch, but there was no systematic work being done on the philosophy of Marxism; of historical and dialectical materialism, of Marxist economics, of the relationship between state and capitalism, on imperialism, on political economy, of the leading role of the Party and its work in the working class.

As the months rolled by, I reluctantly began to see the depth of crisis that had so infected the Party. I was reluctant because I wanted things to be better than they were or could possibly be. This was a failing on my part. I had, in the past, been quick to find fault and I had made up my mind to accept Party discipline. But, on an almost daily basis, the problems emerged, and became glaringly obvious.

The past is rarely spoken of in CPA circles. Those who leave are lost to memory. I discovered that this had also moved into the physical history of the Party. On a couple of occasions, I mentioned to comrades in Melbourne about some momentous events in our history. There was a deep and alarming ignorance of the history of the Party and virtually no curiosity. Nobody that I spoke with had any knowledge of one of the defining moments in the Party's recent history – the Fourth Congress, or the split that followed it. One leading member of the branch, with seven, or, eight years membership, thought I was talking about the split in the old CPA which led to the formation of the SPA! The leading cadre in the branch had been around at that very time but he had not seemed to think it appropriate to educate the membership about these events.

The majority of members of the Melbourne branch are young. This is a good thing but I wondered about just what had happened to long standing members. Communists do not, as a rule, simply disappear. They tend to die in the saddle, unless something compels them to leave. The Melbourne membership is almost exclusively made up of members with less than five years' time in the Party. This should mean that the history ought and must be shared. But it is ignored and no-one seemed concerned or showed the slightest interest in knowing anything about the Party. They all knew of its hundred years of struggle but nothing about the last 40 years!

I still clung to a false and fading hope that Melbourne was an aberration, despite the fact that the General-Secretary was a member of the branch. I had convinced myself that Sydney was in better shape. But then, the signs began to emerge. Branches had collapsed or had been combined. There was virtually no activity in the working-class Western suburbs.

This, combined with so many issues ended with my decision to leave. The moment of decision came six months before my final and formal resignation but it was a moment that left less room for doubt. It was the day of the branch Annual General Meeting. These occasions are significant and symbolic in the life of the Party. This meeting was bookended by a series of emails I had with the editor of the Party's theoretical journal, the *Australian Marxist Review*. I was waiting for the train to take me to Melbourne for the meeting. I had written a piece on the question of left and right opportunism. It used the history of the Party but also spoke in broad terms about the world movement. I didn't think it was all that controversial. The editor was not going to accept the article, saying that he thought the *Guardian* a more appropriate place for it. I replied asking why an article on theory was not suitable for a theoretical journal but hoping for anything like a satisfactory answer was just wishful thinking.

The train trip from Geelong to Melbourne takes an hour and ten minutes. An exchange of emails took the entire time. Each message carried a little more political heat. We were nowhere finished when the train pulled into Melbourne's Southern Cross station. The discussion was not over. The meeting was next on my agenda. The return journey saw the email 'discussion' of theory continue. It was clear that differences of opinion were not to be tolerated. The Party Constitution might speak of criticism and self-criticism. In reality it is a one-way street. A little while back I re-read the article. Yes, it was critical, but surely a theoretical journal is expected to be about theory and surely theory is tested in polemic and 'comradely' debate. I was clearly mistaken. That was the last time we spoke.

I got to the Party AGM and by the meeting's end I was ready to open a vein. The AGM is special, but not this one.

Almost nobody in attendance had paid their dues and so most didn't get their Party cards re-issued. Card re-issue is, or should have been, something of a ceremony. Instead, the General-Secretary who doubles as branch Secretary, tossed them across the table, a bit like a casino croupier but without the style. He gave no official report, which ought to be central to an AGM, opting for a rambling off the cuff talk of trade union and Palestinian solidarity. His reason for not giving a report was because he had been a 'bit busy.' There was a vague comment about the parlous state of financial affairs both nationally and in Victoria. There was no financial report, only the idea that' things aren't good' and that if anyone wanted to know anything specific it would be best to go to him after the meeting and ask. Nobody did.

It was around this time that I became aware of numbers of stalwart comrades in Sydney who had led the struggle for decades had left the Party because they simply felt that it could not be 'saved.' A group of these, former leading cadres in the Party had finally taken the step of creating a new party to build and maintain a Marxist-Leninist presence in Australia. They had formed the New Communist Party of Australia. What had happened? What had gone so terribly wrong?

A COMMUNIST'S JOURNEY

The long march to the marsh

The CPA is a party that is firmly in the grip of opportunist politics and practices. It denies this and asserts that it is simply anti-sectarian and wishes to achieve unity and accord with as wide a spread of left and progressive forces as possible. While this sounds a worthy aim it is not happening and even if it were successful, the theoretical perspectives that make a Marxist-Leninist party what it is, would by necessity be weakened to accommodate 'all flowers.' What happens in reality is that the opportunist party, for the sake of unity, all but disappears.

Under such conditions communists fall behind the trade union leadership and advance few if any demands beyond those of solidarity and often these are made in such a manner as to hide their light under a bushel. We see this in the practice of the CPA today. Let us use May Day as an example but any mass action can be substituted. A small group of Party members will present themselves and the Party colours. More will absent themselves, choosing to march with their respective unions. The union contingents will have no idea that such solidarity has been expressed. Any observer will, if they look hard enough, see a tiny clutch of people holding a CPA banner. But solidarity will have been expressed.

The working class remains locked in a not so tender an embrace with union leaderships that are often not quite up to the mark. There is acceptance of anything that comes from the mouths of the ACTU leadership and so, therefore, remain tied to social democracy and the ALP. The role of communists must be more than this and yet, for fear of being labelled sectarian, no political crime is too much to endure or accept. That is the 'positive' side of things. The working class remains leaderless. The workers do not become class conscious. A mad cycle is repeated and with each repetition the class remain isolated and apolitical.

At the same time identity politics emerges and offers the opportunist a chance to make some imagined gains. Identity as a political issue has been growing as the crisis in the capitalist system has intensified. The opportunist fails to recognise one important aspect in all this. The ruling class doesn't repress these movements. They tolerate them and use them as 'pressure-cooker' valves.

The fact that the CPA has joined the queue, joined the march to embrace identity as a political vehicle, can only have come about as a result of a virtual abandonment of theory and analysis. But such is the sad truth.

Identity, as a political expression must be understood and not simply from a desire to see justice done to those who are marginalised. It is a political expression. It is a philosophical outlook. Marxists must look beyond façades. They must look at society, its relationships and interrelationships, what are the class issues behind things and never retreat from the exhortation of Marx that it is not enough to interpret the word that we must change it. Real change can only come from replacing the economic order of capitalism with socialism.

No matter how appealing the argument, identity cannot replace that greater identity; class. The seemingly irresistible rise of identity came after WWII and the stabilisation of capitalism. Buoyant economies allowed for seemingly harmonious relationships between employer and worker. People were still aware of injustice and sought ways and means of promoting causes that would fight for a just world. It was just that class was declared to be no longer the answer. Enter the politics of identity.

Political movements can be separated into class-based or non-class based. Identity politics as a non-class movement have built strong constituencies. This is an obvious fact. It has achieved concessions from state institutions, but has not eroded state power or the dictatorship of capitalism. Herein lies the rub. If capitalism is the problem, then capitalism ought to be the primary target. Whatever the focus of a campaign defined by identity, it simply does not and nor can it challenge the basic premise of capitalism. This is not to suggest that the issues that identity politics clothes itself in are not important. They all identify issues that are symptomatic of the ills of capitalist society. They are all issues that mark out a society as one that privileges one group over another but are all issues that might as easily be regarded as human rights issues that can be resolved without the economic and political system being challenged in the slightest.

This is not intended to sound mean-spirited. Those engaging in any range of identity politics campaigns do so from the best and noblest of motives. They want change. There will be victories, even if sometimes short-lived, but capitalism will not have lost an inch of ground. Just struggles around all, or any of the issues of the day, can be waged by those espousing an anti-capitalist program, by social-democrats, or equally by conservative politicians. We might remember that marriage equality was won in Australia after the conservative government introduced legislation for it. Tony Blair introduced Britain's Human Rights Act. The Civil Rights Act of 1964 in the US became law under Lyndon Johnson. Change was brought about and has been brought about so many times, but capitalism and its state remain comfortably in place.

Another aspect of identity as a political expression is that there is a tendency to shrink issues, or relegate some issues to the sidelines, or to create enemy camps within the world of identity. This is almost to be expected as this or that 'campaign' is either won, or a new and more radical issue consumes the radical audience's attention. The women's movement, as an example was once so obviously a class-issue and still is. In the hands of the identity politician a process of reduction goes on. The call for equal rights was a class demand. Today, the feminist movement fractures around those who fight for transgender rights and those who do not. At each turn the identity political movement becomes a more exclusive and more 'radical' expression. Rather than building constituencies, a splintering occurs.

The CPA has taken on board many of the trappings of identity politics, just as it has slipped into entrenched opportunist political atrophy. Comrades with decades of commitment to struggle and to theoretical understanding have left the Party. In a vain attempt to remain relevant the CPA has become something quite unlike a fighting Marxist-Leninist organisation.

LOOKING FOR 'HOME'

Some months after I re-joined the Party, an article appeared in the *Guardian*, extolling the virtues and merits of 'Queer Marxism.' Nobody reacted. Nobody questioned. A theorist once said, not altogether in jest, that there were a 1000 Marxisms. There are not. There is Marxism and a thousand deviations from Marxism. It is not a question of picking and choosing to suit a personal taste. We cannot have a smorgasbord approach. When we are told that there is Black Marxism, or Marxist feminism, or Eco-Marxism, or post-Marxist Marxism, or as I had the misfortune to read in a plug for a conference, post-human Marxism, then we can see the mire in which a perfectly sound and rational theory has been dragged.

The Party seems to have lost the capacity to look critically at anything. Sure, there will be critiques of capitalism and exposures of the myriad crimes committed by capitalism, but any statement from any other Communist Party that is held in esteem cannot be questioned. It is almost a matter of letting our 'betters and elders' do the thinking for us. This has certainly been the case with regard to China and the Communist Party of China (CPC). Surely political parties must have the right to disagree. But that would seem to be a blasphemy!

A COMMUNIST'S JOURNEY

The CPA and its China syndrome

The CPA has accepted, without question, the argument that China is not only 'building' socialism but that it is already socialist. A leading CPA 'theorist' waved away any critique of China's position by writing that if you want to know what is happening in China, ask the Chinese. That sounds plausible enough but the 'Chinese' he was urging comrades to consult with were apparently to be found in the editorial offices of the *People's Daily*.

I have been guilty of promoting the 'China is socialist' argument. While writing for the *Guardian*, I wrote frequent 'good news' pieces on China. However, what were at first tiny, unspecified doubts began to surface and to grow. I suffered, as so many others have suffered, from the subjective pushing the objective into the shade. There came a time when those nagging little thoughts needed to be explored. The *People's Daily* might disagree but that's what we, as Marxists, are called upon to do.

There are times when the CPC make statements that are so outrageous as to make any Marxist shake their head in wonderment. Exploitation of the working class, according to the CPC, is permitted, up until the beginning stage of communism. Now communism comes after the defeat of capitalism, after the initial stages of socialist construction, and after the creation of a fully operational socialist economy and social system. By this stage the state will have withered away, class divisions will have disappeared and then, and only then will come communism. By any stretch of the imagination, that time is a long way off. While there is exploitation of the working class there can be no movement toward anything like socialism. It is an absurd notion. Class divisions must reduce and be eliminated. That is the job of the Revolution. It is the task of socialism, even in its earliest and most backward stages. The Soviet experience, for all its faults, prided itself on the undeniable fact that the workers were not enriching a capitalist class. But that is precisely what is happening in China today.

Capitalism can only survive and grow by exploitation. Profits are made by extracting surplus value from the labour of the working class. This is at the very basis of Marxism and yet the CPC can justify class exploitation. The CPA and a number of other communist parties are happy to shut their eyes and close their ears to such truths.

The Chinese Constitution was, quite recently, amended. It guarantees in law, the right of private capitalism to exist in China. We are not talking of small-scale businesses but of major capitalist enterprises. Chinese state labour laws declare that the working day shall not exceed eight hours and that the working week shall be no more than 40 hours. Today Chinese capitalists openly flout these laws. What is worse is that many of these 'entrepreneurs' and private operators are members of the Chinese Party. The worst examples are in the infamous 9-9-6 contracts. Under these 'illegal' but open contracts, workers must be on the job from 9:00am-9:00pm, six days a week. This adds up to 72 hours a week! Home grown Chinese employers use these contracts and so too do foreign exploiters. Elon Musk runs factories in Shanghai on the 9-9-6 formula. The CPA ignores this. China is socialist. The mantra must not be interrupted. An old joke revolved around a communist speaker in Sydney's Hyde Park. It was the 1930s. A heckler kept throwing curly questions about problems in the Soviet Union. Each was batted away with 'but they're building socialism.' Finally, the heckler shouted, 'they eat their babies.' The speaker paused for a moment and said 'yes, but they're building socialism.' It was a joke. The CPA is living the joke.

My former comrades in my branch were derisive of any report from any source that was even marginally critical of China. It was hardly edifying. To be fair, I can well remember being very defensive of the Soviet Union and quick to denounce 'anti-Soviet propaganda' but what I was witnessing was in a league of its own.

LOOKING FOR 'HOME'

A hotch-potch of ideas

At about the time that I began this memoir, a post appeared on the CPA's Victorian Facebook page. It was still there when I was finishing. It is a link to an interview with a leading figure in the Communist Party of Great Britain (Marxist-Leninist). The interview was all about discounting any notion that China might possibly be an imperialist power and also that Russia could not be considered as imperialist. There is nothing special about that. Many of the CPA's closest allies hold that view. For the CPA it is a truth that cannot and must not be argued against. What made the post interesting was the fact that the CPGB (ML) adopted, just a year or two earlier, a position denouncing identity politics in general and LGBTQI+ 'ideology as reactionary and anti-working class.' It seems that nobody in the CPA had actually read anything beyond the pro-China material interview. The CPGB (ML) go further, stating that any member promoting such issues and especially transgender issues will be expelled from the Party!

Given the near unanimous support that these issues enjoy on the left, the CPGB (ML) found itself in the middle of a furious debate. The rights or wrongs of that debate are best put aside. The CPA is a strong advocate of LGBTQI+ rights and promotes them whenever possible. The same people who are leading the charge for 'trans-rights' in the CPA appear happy to support a party that they would otherwise deride as 'reactionary' or possibly 'fascist.' They both support and are blind to any criticism of China. The CPA members have not read anything but blithely post articles from a communist party without thought and with no knowledge of that party's policies. What is extraordinary is that not one of the members seem to have noticed!

This hotch-potch of ideas is overseen by leading Party members. There are almost no pre-conditions on joining the Party. It had long been a practice within the SPA and later the CPA that prospective members should be brought, carefully into full membership. It was a requirement that the prospective recruit must attend a series of classes, work with other branch members, sell the paper and find out just what it is to become a communist. Each month, while I was with the CPA, there would be at least one membership application to be ratified. This should have been encouraging. The application would be summarily given the all-clear. Frequently, that was the last anyone saw or heard of the recruit.

The branch communicates, via an in-house chat group on Telegram. The numbers of those on the list never seemed to vary, although the applications for membership kept being ratified. Nobody seemed perturbed by this.

LOOKING FOR 'HOME'

About three months after I re-joined, two young comrades, who joined at about the same time, asked in a meeting about setting up a fraction. The LGBTQI+ fraction was born. Each meeting of the branch would hear reports from fractions. For the most part these reports were never delivered, due to the fact that there was nothing to report.

Theory drives practice and practice tests theory. There is nothing extraordinary about that. The CPA leadership maintain that a strong ideological current defines the work of the Party. Statements are routinely made at various levels of the hierarchy that the work must be conducted in a non-sectarian manner. All this is well and good. Whatever work that gets done is so carefully 'non-sectarian' as to render it invisible.

Two issues captured the imagination, if not all the energy of the Party throughout 2024. The genocide in Gaza and the assault on the CFMEU by State and Federal governments alike. The first of these, the Israeli invasion of Gaza, saw mobilisations across the country that were simply astonishing. The Party newspaper covered the war in every issue for that year, and beyond. The Central Committee urged all Party organisations to attend the rallies. In Melbourne this meant a tiny group of members attending the rallies every week. When a trade union solidarity group for Palestine was organised, Party members who were trade union members tended to join their unions rather than march under the Party banner. From time-to-time comrades would use Telegram to ask where the Party contingent was. The thought never occurred to the branch executive to nominate a gathering point or to organise beyond a vague call to attend. There were few, and by this I must stress very few leaflets produced, which were mostly re-prints of *Guardian* articles. There were no public meetings held and there was one stand-alone rally organised by the Party branch. This attracted five Party members.

The other big issue for that year was the attack on the CFMEU. This was uppermost in discussion and in reports to the branch. The rallies in Melbourne were huge. The Party presence was, once more, embarrassing. I counted five of us among a demonstration of well over 20,000. A banner had been produced for this specific purpose but for some reason was not taken, even though the march kicked off from Trades Hall where the CPA office was located. There was one placard held by the General-Secretary, two others handed out a few leaflets and two of us distributed *Guardians*. Yet another signpost.

An issue that exercised the minds and Telegram chatters was the altogether regrettable and resistible rise of the far-right. The National Socialist Network occupied a lot of time (on the chat-line) but was never once raised in a Party meeting. No leaflets were written, no rallies organised, no public meetings called in the name of the Party. All I can imagine was that any overt action by the Party would be dismissed by the leadership and by the membership as 'sectarian.'

It was all so depressing. When I came back to the Party, I did so with no particular illusions or expectations. I accepted that the CPA was in reduced circumstances, that the ideological level would be weak and uneven, and that the crisis of the 21st century individualist mentality would have become present in the Party. I pushed all this to one side. This was how things were, but even so I held to a vain hope that better days would come. After all the crisis of capitalism was and is so deep. Lives have been made so wretched, the threat of poverty, anxiety, alienation, of inequality, the threat of war and climate catastrophe meant, in my imagination, that the Marxist-Leninist forces would not only rise to the occasion but win hearts and minds. I was wrong.

The final straw came, by accident. I learned, and not through any official Party channel, that Spiro Anthony had died. Spiro, who had given his life to the struggle for a socialist future, was dead. Spiro, who had sat in our flat in Moscow, eating all that Beluga caviar that 'would not last' had died and his death had been ignored by the Party. Spiro had waged a long struggle inside the Party. He fought for the values of Marxism-Leninism and, in the end, accepted that the CPA was beyond redemption and left.

The final straw, was not so much that he had felt it necessary to break from the CPA, or that his closest allies, several of whom were members of the CPA Central Committee left with him and soon after formed a new organisation; the New Communist Party of Australia. It was that by resigning his membership he had become a 'non-person.' He had pursued knowledge and theoretical understanding for decades and he had now been airbrushed from history.

I took the decision to leave the CPA but not immediately. As 2025 began, I knew it would be my last year with the CPA. A Party Congress was coming. I knew that I probably would not last for the year but thought I would hang on until June or July to take part in the pre-Congress discussions. I couldn't.

My last act as a member of the Communist Party of Australia was to write an opinion-piece for the Guardian that criticised some of the Party's positions regarding China, Russia, of what was or was not Imperialism and pointing out that debate and polemic was, in fact a healthy thing. I also wrote a lengthy statement of resignation that I sent to the CPA General-Secretary and Central Committee a few days before May Day. It seemed, somehow, to be an apt timing to make such a symbolic gesture. But what happens next?

Chapter Seven

Not the end: just another part of the journey

What happens next? There is always a 'next' and it is what keeps us all moving. It is a motivating factor and something that separates humanity from other animals. Things are not neatly packaged. There is always a beginning and certainly a middle but an end? Human evolution is on-going. Societal developments, economic formations, political structures are never static. This is at the very centre of Marxist theory.

Historical materialism, the term coined by Engels, is based in economic change and how class relations change. It shows just how society has been in constant flux; how entire economic formations come into life, flower and are replaced by new formations that drive us forward. As it is with the history of the world, so too can it be seen in the life of any one of us.

NOT THE END: JUST ANOTHER PART OF THE JOURNEY

Life is often depicted in literature, on screen, on the stage. At the end of the book, film or play, there is an ending, either a happy, satisfactory ending or an unsatisfactory ending, but it is rare that the characters have a life beyond the last chapter, or scene. There can be a beauty in knowing that life and art are not entirely synonymous. There is always another chapter to our story. I take great heart from that.

Many years ago, I worked in theatre. At the end of a children's pantomime, the cast met with the children while their buses loaded them for a return to their various schools. A little girl, about five years-old was sobbing. A couple of us went to try and comfort her. She could not be comforted. She told us that she wanted to stay and see what happened next! When I was sending a lengthy letter and statement of resignation to the Communist Party of Australia, that image returned to me. What happens next?

Marx once wrote that 'men make their own history, but they do not make it under circumstances chosen by themselves, but under circumstances directly encountered, given and transmitted from the past.' The wisdom is obvious. While we seek to shape our lives, those lives are shaped, not in isolation, but are influenced, constrained and developed by historical and social conditions. This has huge implications for those seeking not simply to interpret the world but to change it. It also has implications for the individual.

My life has followed a path not always of my choosing. Nobody's does. When I was young and stumbled upon socialist politics, I accepted it without any real notion of what life might have in store. I have heard of people who have consciously mapped out a life and ticked off the pre-planned stages. They are, I believe, oddities. I knew such a one when I was a student and student activist. He was already a man on a mission. Join the Young Liberals, complete studies, join the Liberal Party, begin practising law, get Party preselection, go into parliament, join the cabinet. Fortunately, there are very few that come so single-minded, so focussed, so driven.

I suppose the young Liberal and I, each in our own way, 'made our own history.' I certainly did not make mine under circumstances chosen by myself, but 'under circumstances directly encountered, given and transmitted from the past.' Marx and Marxism have always enabled me to make sense of my life and of the world in which I live.

Marx's wisdom makes sense of my life. Engels' description of the process of history gives me stability, just as it has for those thousands of communists who have struggled in this country and the millions across the world who have listened to, read, and understood the truths of our theory. Without that, life would be pointless, meaningless, and we would be blown like chaff before the wind.

Yes, I stumbled upon socialism, but I was receptive to its call. It seemed right then and it is right now. The only difference is that the need for socialism is greater than at any time in our history. And it is because that need is greater that communists must fight so much harder to equip the working class to become class conscious, to help them realise their strength, so they might organise against capitalism and break the shackles. Any retreat from the working class under these conditions is a betrayal. It is a betrayal of the working class. It is a betrayal of Marx, Engels, Lenin. It is a betrayal of an idea that can and will save the world. So many political organisations that clothe themselves in Marxist attire have turned away from the class struggle. Oh, lip service will be paid, but their real place is amid the marsh of identity politics and the politics that can be served by any variation of social democracy. I believe myself to be after all these years, a communist, a Marxist-Leninist, and so must stand for what I truly believe and never settle for second best.

This is why I joined the communist movement and this is why I left the Communist Party of Australia

A clean break

A public resignation from the CPA is all but impossible. Ranks close rapidly. The person or persons who make such a break are simply no longer referred to. For the Party it is a clean break, even if it hides from the view of the membership that there are problems.

While knowing this to be the case, I prepared a lengthy resignation letter. It was my 'clean break.' I have no knowledge if any but a very select few read it or even if it was read in its entirety. It is too long to be reproduced here. It focused on what a communist party ought to be about. I offered a brief critique of how the Party had in all but name, departed from the cause of Marxism-Leninism. It sought to describe the debilitating consequences that came with the chipping away of core elements of Marxist theory that took place across the 20th century. It highlighted the tragedy that was and is neoliberal ideology and the shattering of the idea of the collective in favour of the individual and how that has become evident in the way the CPA and the left in general respond to the crisis of capitalism.

The act of resignation concluded with these few paragraphs:

> 'I remain committed to the ideology of Marxism-Leninism; an ideology that has framed

NOT THE END: JUST ANOTHER PART OF THE JOURNEY

the lives and thinking of so many thousands of comrades before me who have worked so long and so hard for a socialist Australia. While I am leaving the CPA, I believe I am remaining true to the memories of those courageous comrades. I believe that the Party has not ...

The leadership of the Party have permitted it to become a shell of its former self. I do not speak in terms of membership figures. That is less significant than how the membership is armed and equipped for struggle. Older comrades who have sat by and allowed this disintegration to take place are as much at fault as any 'ideologically' motivated cadre that has driven the CPA into opportunism and demoralisation. Many a comrade has left over the years. Their contributions have often been huge and yet, even in death, they are treated as if they never existed. This is shameful.

For all these reasons I can no longer consider myself a member of the CPA. I will remain a communist, a Marxist-Leninist and maintain a firm belief in and commitment to the struggle for socialism. My faith in the working class as the only force capable of effecting Revolutionary change remains undiminished.'

Good fortune

I count myself among the fortunate. A number of chance events led me to this moment in my life. It is all a case of roads not travelled, but there have been some very significant roads that I did travel.

In 1971, a chance encounter with a left-wing paper seller changed the trajectory of my life and gave that young life the beginnings of purpose. A chance meeting with an old friend who encouraged me to complete my secondary education gave me entry to a new world. Meeting Rose was undoubtedly the best bit of luck. I found not only my future wife and companion but a comrade with whom to share the journey. A casual invitation to a meeting brought me into contact with some of the finest individuals that anyone could meet. The debt that I owe to those old communists; Lenny Brown, Alex Randall, George Chenery, and through them to the many fine men and women that helped shape my life, is huge.

Finding the SPA, joining the Party, becoming active, being offered the job in Moscow, were all acts of great good fortune. My horizons broadened, my understanding of politics deepened and slowly I began to not simply be that straw that is blown upon the wind. Good luck enabled me to make decisions, or at least I allowed decisions to be made for me.

The years spent in the Soviet Union changed me more than I could realise. I had the great privilege to have lived and worked in a socialist world and can state, hand on heart, that for all of its problems and shortcomings, the socialist Soviet Union offered far more than life under capitalism. I felt a liberation of the spirit. This is opposed to the crushing of the spirit that we all of us encounter every day of our lives.

As the years passed, experience, and piece by piece, the acquisition of a theoretical and ideological armour has allowed me to make decisions, consciously and with some sense of authority.

What had been building along the journey was 'polished' to an extent by my return to full-time study. I was able to test the theory that meant so much to me. Few, if any of my lecturers shared my views. I was told that Marx was dead and so why bother? Others expressed a belief in 'radical social-democracy.' By the time I completed my studies, I had proven something, if not to anyone else, then at least to myself. The 'reader' and assessor of my PhD thesis that was unashamedly a defence of Marxism had dismissed it as an attempt to 'clarify the author's own thoughts.' I did clarify those thoughts.

This reflection of a journey; a communist's journey, to Moscow and beyond, is only possible because of those first 'lucky breaks' and while the journey has not always been a smooth one, I would not have chosen any other course. When faced with what seemed almost impossible odds, Alex would simply say, 'we've got time on our side.' Lenny once wondered aloud about what would happen with the USA, the Cold War and the potential for nuclear destruction. 'If we have a Revolution before other capitalist countries, the Yanks will just nuke us. If we are the last to go, then they'll probably make a last stand and we'll be nuked. Only one thing for it. Keep struggling.' Len's simple logic holds true. Keep struggling.

NOT THE END: JUST ANOTHER PART OF THE JOURNEY

Leaving the CPA was able to be achieved without any sense of regret. It was the end of something, but really just the end of a chapter. The story continues. The journey is by no means over. There will come a time when my personal journey will end. It is intensely unlikely that I will see the victory of the working class and the beginnings of socialism in this country. That personally is of little consequence. The victory will still come. What is important is, as Lenny said, to 'keep struggling', to fight with whatever weapons you might have at your disposal for a future that will bring dignity, fulfilment, hope and a better world. To fight against a world that exploits labour, that enriches the few at the expense of the many, that perpetuates greed, inequality, despair, that drives people mad, that promotes hatred, war and the devastation of our planet, is a fight worth the effort.

The little girl outside the theatre, all those years ago wanted to know what happens next. For communists, for Marxist-Leninists, what happens next is the building of a political party that is prepared to stand with the working class, that is prepared to develop a strong theoretical base upon which to build, that is prepared to fight and win.

www.ingramcontent.com/pod-product-compliance
Lightning Source LLC
Chambersburg PA
CBHW022057290426
44109CB00014B/1130